"People Leave Managers...Not Organizations"

"What a great book! You have successfully combined an individual and organizational road map to success. *People Leave Managers...Not Organizations* allows leaders to self diagnosis challenges and then provides a concise action plan that promotes shared success. The most powerful organizations share a common vision, embrace guidelines not rules, and focus on the results not the methods. Each of these principals is highlighted and supported in your work."

Rick Frederico
Chairman/CEO, P. F. Changs

"Finally a book that can help all managers where we need it the most....cultivating collaborative and productive relationships with the people we lead, which will in turn drive improved results! I don't think anyone in a position of responsibility to others and accountable for results can afford not to read this book."

Art Smuck
Vice President, ATC Logistics & Electronics

"People routinely ask us in Nucor how they can replicate our incentive system so they can get the same type of results. I always tell those folks that our bonus doesn't create those results; it's the right people in the right environment. Leaders create that environment and this book offers a how-to approach describing the actions leaders need to take. This approach is a manager's operating manual to continually improve its most important assets. It is now a part of Nucor's leadership development efforts."

Dan Krug
Manager Employee Relations, Nucor Corporation

D1114572

"I've been using Rick Tate's approaches to leadership and customer service for 20 years. Because his methods are heavily-grounded in common-sense and reality, they WORK! I'm pleased that he and Dr. Julie White are now addressing the issues of performance management with the same common-sense and reality. Using their methods will make this often-difficult management responsibility much easier, in both the private sector and in government."

Bill Wade
Past Superintendent, National Park Service

"This may very well be the best book ever written on effective performance management!"

Bob Nelson Ph.D.
President, Nelson Motivation Inc.
Best-selling author of *1001 Ways to Reward Employees*,

People Leave Managers…Not Organizations!

People Leave Managers...Not Organizations!

Action Based Leadership

Rick Tate and Dr. Julie White

iUniverse, Inc.

New York Lincoln Shanghai

People Leave Managers...Not Organizations!
Action Based Leadership

iUniverse books may be ordered through booksellers or by contacting:

iUniverse
2021 Pine Lake Road, Suite 100
Lincoln, NE 68512
www.iuniverse.com
1-800-Authors (1-800-288-4677)

ISBN: 0-595-33168-8 (Pbk)
ISBN: 0-595-77976-X (Cloth)

Printed in the United States of America

Table of Contents

Foreword

By Bob Nelson, Ph.D.

Rarely does one find so much management wisdom condensed in a single work! Rick and Julie distill the challenges of management we have all seen, experienced and, yes, grappled with, into a pithy, fresh and insightful narrative rarely found in business books today. Behind every principle or insight is a story that captures the essence of the challenge—fun to read, yet painful to remember the similar situations and blunders you may well have faced on your own management journey. Now you can face similar situations with a new sense of confidence—even excitement—knowing that, with Rick and Julie's guidance, you can now get it right!

Time after time, you'll find yourself nodding as Rick and Julie expose arcane organizational practices that have perhaps become permanent fixtures in your own workplace, now laid bare for all to see the limitations and silliness we've been blind to before. As a storyteller extraordinaire, Rick's skill in capturing the moment, honing the truth, and illuminating the learnings comes through on almost every page.

This book gets to the core of what every employee knows to be true: If you have a good boss, you have a good job! Since employees report that four out of five managers they have had in their career have not been that good, this is a point well worth exploring. We each tend to remember the good managers we've had and think twice or more before ever leaving such a manager.

Most managers manage in the way they have been managed in the course of their own career. For most of us, it is our first manager that leaves a lasting imprint on how we approach the job of managing. Rick and Julie show us there is a better way and that following their path will lead to better results for both you and your employees. With their Performance Advantage Method they give us a model that serves as both diagnostic tool and roadmap for dealing with performance challenges of your employees. It is a practical framework for both managing and continually improving performance.

The concept of the organization is an abstract one. A good company may very well be a draw to attract people to your firm. But whether they stay, and whether they do their best is today more a function of how people are treated in their jobs. As I've always said, "There's a big difference between getting people to come to work and getting them to do their best work!"

If you want work to matter to your people, you have to give them a reason to care, to show them that their best efforts are, indeed, needed and that each employee's contribution does, in fact, make a difference. When it comes to real estate, the adage may be "location, location, location," but when in comes to motivation, the adage is "relationships, relationships, relationships." And it's the relationship with one's manager that matters the most in helping us each attain the performance of which we are capable.

Rick and Julie make the case that when the day is done, its performance that matters the most in motivating any employee. As a manager creates a work environment that inspires employees to new heights of performance, they will in turn become a magnet for talent. People who perform well, feel good about themselves, and are most likely to perform even better, taking on new challenges along the way!

Thank you, Rick and Julie, for helping to take the guesswork out of managing! This may very well be the best book ever written on effective performance management!

—Bob Nelson, Ph.D.
President, Nelson Motivation Inc.
Best-selling Author, *1001 Ways to Reward Employees,*
The Management Bible, and *Managing For Dummies*

Preface

Consider retention. Having good performers leave your organization hurts performance results. But even worse than having talented people who quit and leave is having employees who "quit and stay"!

Attracting, developing, and retaining talented employees is the theme of this book. And make no mistake; people do leave managers, not organizations.

We have been in the business of performance management and leadership effectiveness for over two decades. Beyond graduate degrees in organizational behavior, leadership, counseling, and women's studies, we have over 50 years of experience in managerial roles and working with organizations on performance improvement and leadership/management improvement efforts. Through these efforts we have gained substantial insights to many facets of organizational performance issues. We have been on both sides; as practicing managers and as consultants, trainers, and change agents.

Over the years we have conducted numerous organizational assessments and conducted thousands of interviews with managers and employees. The stories we have heard and the issues we have been privy to have shaped our thinking in very profound ways. Performance management difficulties range from complex misunderstandings of human motivation at work to blinding flashes of the obvious; that is, common sense on the lam. The performance management lessons we have acquired are presented in this book with the hope and expectation that others may benefit and accelerate their competence in the art of managing people.

From our experience it is clear that the relationship between the manager and the employee is the overriding factor in both the employee's quality of performance and the employee's quality of work life. Our personal experience validates this point, our research and assessments with many organizations underscores our experience, and the research in the performance management field supports this premise.

Work with our clients ranging from Disney to Cargill, from both private and public sector organizations, from mid range companies to start-ups indicate the challenge for managers is clear. Performance management excellence is dependent on *skill* acquisition. Over the years we have observed that a predictable way of dealing with poor performance management issues is to develop and implement a new performance appraisal or evaluation system. Other times we have seen management teams tinker with the compensation system. While system issues are certainly critical and their alignment with performance excellence is paramount, we have never seen an improvement in performance management without the acquisition and improvement in the human relations skills that support effective leadership. Any system is in jeopardy when the participants in the system lack the skill sets necessary to make the system work.

It's problematic that the influence, communication, confrontation, and leadership skills that are necessary for effective performance management are not acquired through normal educational processes. It is often noted that we learn more about dealing with facts, figures, and machines than we do about how to interact and effectively deal with other human beings. However, these necessary skills can be learned and applied. When these skills are learned within the context of a replicable method, continuous improvement can be realized.

In Chapter 1 and Chapter 2 we discuss the impact of motivation and leadership in the workplace and the impact on performance. We start by taking a critical look at many of the traditional and commonplace motivational techniques that seem to have very little positive influence on performance issues. From our experience we look at the unintended consequences of well intentioned, yet ineffective leadership practices.

In Chapters 3 through 7 we construct our Performance Advantage Method. Using a decision tree process we construct a replicable model that mangers can utilize to deal effectively with performance issues. It is clear that for lack of a method, many mangers manage performance as a series of events, with each individual event stimulating a managerial reaction. A more pro-active approach is necessary if managers are to achieve mastery in the art of performance management.

In Chapter 3 we deal with the issue of performance expectations. Over and over we are enlightened by commentary from our client base and from substantial research in the area of performance management to the fact that many problem performance issues are the result of unclear or misaligned performance expectations. We provide the reader with a clearer understanding of how performance expectations can become ambiguous and unclear and some ideas to put in place to clarify and align performance expectations.

In Chapter 4 we take on the issue of ability difficulties. Many times we encounter managers who try to inspire performance with a 'rah-rah' approach when it is an issue of ability deficiencies. The consequences of (1) failing to provide structure and training when necessary, or (2) disciplining in any way performance failures when ability deficiency is the issue can be problematic for any organization. In this book we examine the appropriate manager action when employee ability is the issue.

In Chapter 5 we identify those performance situations where employee confidence determines the performance outcome. Mis-diagnosing performance situations and overlooking how confidence affects employee behavior can result in strained relationships between manager and employee. The relevant leadership action is reviewed and action plans are provided for dealing with employee confidence issues.

In Chapter 6 employee commitment is considered. Many times performance is below what is doable because employees have lost their commitment to do their best. The reasons are varied, but commitment issues are not dealt with effectively with traditional carrot and stick methods. The underlying cause must be uncovered and addressed in a positive manner. These underlying causes to commitment issues are explored and appropriate leadership actions are provided.

In Chapter 7 we take a look at how to effectively handle situations where there is lack of employee motivation or desire. For many managers, dealing with these types of attitudinal problems are difficult encounters. We take a look at the causes of lack of desire in the workplace and offer a variety of approaches to counteract the loss of motivation.

In Chapter 8 the issue of employee initiative is addressed. Over the years one of the challenges for managers is how to create initiative and personal responsibility in the workplace. With the nature of competition in today's world and the requirements for organizations to be not only accurate in how things are done but fast and responsive as well, a dependent performance culture is a competitive disadvantage. We will explore a variety of ways to encourage and require initiative and personal responsibility throughout the organization.

In Chapter 9 we discuss the art of effective delegation. To retain talent challenge, responsibility, trust, and personal achievement are characteristics that must be present for employees. Many managers fail at delegation not due to negligence but due to ineffective delegation practices. Allowing opportunities for talented people to stand on their own two feet and feel a sense of significant contribution to the enterprise is a critical competency for any manager. In an era where managers are constantly asked to do more with fewer resources and restricted budgets, an effective remedy is to have talented people who take the initiative and responsibility.

It is our intention that this book will provide some practical insight to the performance management issues managers face and offer many practical suggestions on how to deal effectively with the variety of performance situations they encounter. We also will provide a performance management method that is doable, replicable, useful, and effective. It is our experience that our Performance Advantage Method will improve the performance management competencies for any manager or supervisor who has the responsibility of managing the performance of others.

Enjoy,

Rick Tate & Julie White

Acknowledgements

Like with any work, we are indebted to those who have come before. We have been blessed with the knowledge of significant figures in the discipline of organizational psychology and management development. Some, we have learned from by reading their works while others we have had the pleasure of learning from personally. While we can never cover all those who have made a difference in our thinking we list several here so as to not forget. The classic works of Abraham Maslow, Douglas McGregor, William Oncken, Jr., Chris Argyris, and Warren Bennis stand out for us as significant contributions. More recent works of Marcus Buckingham, Curt Coffman, Ferdinand Fournies, David Berlo, and Russ Linden have been influential in our thinking. We are extremely grateful for the lessons we have learned from those we have been fortunate to interact with and learn from, namely, Paul Hersey, Ken Blanchard, Tom Peters, Robert Nelson, Marshall Goldsmith, Bill Schwarz, Gary Heil, Kerry Patterson, Bill Eastman, William Oncken, III, Ron Campbell, Dan Harrison, Bill Wade, Sam Shriver, and Mike Staver.

People Leave Managers…not Organizations! provides managers at every level with the ability to understand how to take the right action, at the right time, to increase performance and create a motivational work environment. For years, the myth of traditional thinking was that creating high morale resulted in high performance. Think again! Authors Rick Tate and Dr. Julie White destroy this myth and provide managers practical, applied methods, skills, and concepts that come directly from over 30 years of research in organizational effectiveness, not from some new management "flavor of the month." With a concise, easy to remember model, managers will be energized to lead more effectively, with fewer resources and within tighter budgets. Imagine what it will be like to take action…the right action, at the right time to get bottom line results!

People Leave Managers…not Organizations! focuses on the manager's role and actions to impact:

- Employee Motivation
- Performance Expectations
- Employee Ability
- Employee Attitude
- Confidence
- Desire and Motivation
- Organizational Issues
- Personal Issues
- Meaningful Participation
- Leadership Action: When the leader's action is aligned with the follower's performance results and attitude (rather than the leader's comfort zone), then performance, retention, and relationships all improve.

CHAPTER 1

Leadership and Performance

"We'll camp here!"

—Rooster Cogburn, *True Grit*

Saddle Up

For many of us, when the "Duke" rode onto the silver screen and into our childhoods, the moments were memorable. Sure it was playacting, but John Wayne's portrayals showed us our leverage was in our workers and that leadership qualities could mobilize people in a focused effort to produce, to overcome, to change, and to succeed.

We remember the most complicated order the Duke ever gave was "Saddle up!" However, when the order was given, people saddled up. No one complained, no

1

one argued over which horse to take, no one grumbled about why, and there were no hesitations. Today, decision making is deemed a critical leadership skill, and the Duke can be our benchmark. In the movie *True Grit*, he was leading a young woman and a ranger on a mission of considerable importance. Riding along, he drank from a flask and got drunk enough to fall from his horse. As he was lying there in a stupor, his two followers looked over at him. He made eye contact with them and commanded, "We'll camp here." And camp they did!

The Duke's leadership was simple and elegant. The good guys (the good performers) always won, and the bad guys (the poor performers) always lost. If it were only that easy! However, we know that leaders and followers in the real world don't have scripts to guide them that result in mutual success. And in the real world, sometimes the poor performers not only escape being held accountable, but they are allowed to contaminate the workplace. We also know that effective and appropriate leadership and performance management skills remain key factors in determining the quality of performance in an organization. Further, the person an employee reports to has the greatest influence on the quality of work life and employee loyalty.

The obligation of leading and managing people is an awesome responsibility. There are concepts that can be learned and adapted to your own personal style that will inspire outstanding performance. So, "saddle up," and take a journey through the following pages to learn about excellence in leadership and performance management.

People Leave Managers…Not Organizations

At a fundamental level, we have always known that your immediate supervisor or manager plays the *determining* role regarding employee retention and the quality of employee performance. Now we have research to validate those gut-level feelings. Marcus Buckingham and Curt Coffman provided insight into employee productivity and employee retention in their landmark book, *First Break All the Rules*. This insight, based on over twenty-five years of research by the Gallup Organization, identified the relationship between the employee and his or her direct supervisor or manager as the number one influence on how long an employee stays and how productive he or she is. The conclusion is that people leave managers, not organizations!

> *People leave managers...not organizations.* *
> *The manager sets the tone and is the major influence on the employee in the work environment.*

Issues that correlate with employee retention and productivity*

- Performance expectations must be clear

- People must have the resources to do the job right.

- People must be able to make a difference and contribute (do what they do best) every day.

- People must receive recognition for their contributions and efforts.

- People need to be cared about as individuals.

- People must have meaningful participation at work.

- People need others to encourage their growth and development.

- People need leaders/managers who are adaptable to individual follower performance needs.

* *From organizational assessments and manager and employee interviews over the last fifteen years.*

Citing thousands of employees, these authors found links between employee opinion of the work environment and employee tenure, employee productivity, and business unit performance. These links support the breakthrough thinking discussed in the next pages regarding the issues around successful leadership and outstanding employee performance. Also, our organizational assessments over the last fifteen years highly correlate with the issues of what talented employees look for in their jobs.

It is very clear that the issue is the supervisor or manager to whom employees report directly. In this regard, the responsibility of the local supervisor or manager to his or her organization can be daunting. The profound impact of this person on the working life of others and performance possibilities is critical to an organization's success. Practical and effective leadership skills are the lifeblood of the organization.

- * **hook** (hook) *n.* 2 to be fastened or caught by a hook—**hook up** to connect to—**hooked up** connected, linked together, attached; see JOINED. (*Merriam-Webster's Collegiate Dictionary.* 11th ed. Springfield, MA: Merriam-Webster, 2003.)

Throughout this book we will offer "hooks," highlighted in shaded boxes, to connect important ideas and concepts for your immediate recall.

A Method to the Madness

For years, a major complaint in organizations has been the inconsistency or poor quality of leadership and management skills. Our assessments of leadership and management practices in organizations have found a variety of philosophies, ideas, and practices in play. While consulting and training managers, we have found no focused, coherent discussion or dialogue regarding leading people. There are as many opinions and assumptions as there are managers.

When employees move from one department to another or when their manager changes, adapting to the new style and management ways of the new boss occupies the majority of time during the first few months. In many ways, boss watching is the number one sport in organizations. People want to know how to win—that is, how to please the person who has the greatest impact on their work day. The lack of predictability, consistency, and understanding leads to a type of madness that pervades the hallways of our organizations.

> **Boss Watching**
>
> • "How will I be managed now?"
>
> • "How will my performance be evaluated?"
>
> • "What are my manager's expectations?"
>
> • What is it like to work for this person?
>
> These questions are often asked as employees try to figure out the leadership and performance management practices of their supervisors and managers…how to win with their boss!

Perhaps the lack of a method* is responsible. We believe so. The renowned quality expert Edward Deming always advised that, without a method, results are out of control and unpredictable. This is true in any line of work from accounting to engineering to sales. Other disciplines have adopted methods that can be practiced, replicated, and critiqued for improved results. A method allows a degree of discipline and rigor to be applied to skills and talents. To produce better employee performance results, managers need to adopt a method on which they can rely.

• * **method** (meth'əd) *n.* ((<Fr <Gr *meta*, after + *hodos*, a way)) **1.** a way of doing anything: process **2.** a system in doing things or handling ideas (*Merriam-Webster's Collegiate Dictionary.* 11th ed. Springfield, MA: Merriam-Webster, 2003.

One Size Does Not Fit All...But!

There is no best way to lead. One size does not fit all. To think so assumes that everyone who is to be lead is the same. This demeans the individual and restricts the application of his or her strengths. By method we don't mean a rigid set of specific behavioral steps or scripts that managers must follow. Nor do we mean that managers must forego their natural personality styles and strengths. By method we mean a thought process grounded in a set of fundamental principles that provide supervisors and managers with a replicable process when leading people. The key is to learn the method so it can be practiced within the individual styles and personalities that managers possess. The method then is a basic routine to which leaders apply their personal style and strengths, a basic routine that is grounded in principles that correlate with effective performance management.

Shared Language

With a method for leadership and performance management, managers in the organization adopt a common language regarding leading people and managing results. This fosters joint problem solving and teamwork among managers because they have a shared framework to work through performance issues and difficulties. While managers retain their own personality style, they can use the method to stay on the same page when dealing with performance.

Likewise, a method allows managers to share with employees what they can expect regarding leadership and management practices. We have often wondered why managers don't make part of every employee orientation a discussion about what the employee can expect regarding the way the manager manages people and the process the manager uses for managing performance. Again, perhaps it is the lack of a practical method that makes leadership and performance management so ambiguous when it comes to how individual managers lead others.

> **How to Get Along**
>
> - "Do your job well and bring a good attitude and we will get along fine."
> - "Give 100% and we won't have any problems."
> - "Do your best and remember, come to me if you have any problems."
>
> Statements such as these capture the way that many managers articulate to employees what it will be like working for them.

We know that managers will offer employees advice on how they deal with people. However, generic commentaries about "getting along" and "generalized expectations" are the rule. Although these types of statements do offer advice, they do not provide any specifics or give any understanding to the employee regarding *how* the manager manages. The employees cannot take any proactive measures to influence how they are treated by the manager. The employees are constantly reacting to the manager's reactions.

What is needed is the combinations of flexibility and individuality that taps into each manager's strengths and the application of a method for leadership and performance management. Such a method, understood by employees, will allow them to be proactive in their relationship with their manager and in their approach to their own performance objectives.

Performance Management: Condition or Problem?

In medicine, professionals are astute in differentiating between a condition and a problem. Problems, such as a broken bone in the arm, can be fixed. Once completely fixed, no further attention is necessary. On the other hand, a condition, such as asthma, can't be fixed. A condition requires ongoing treatment. The type of treatment changes as the degree of the condition changes. To some degree, a condition requires some type of treatment all of the time.

Most often managers approach performance issues in organizations as though they were problems. Performance problems are the topic of many training programs. The underlying assumption is that performance issues are problems that require fixing. This is a mistake. The performance of individuals and teams in organizations is a condition. The condition of performance at any one

> **Condition or Problem**
>
> Human performance is a condition that requires ongoing treatment, not a problem that can be fixed!

time is the result of a myriad of factors relating to the abilities, attitudes, and cooperation of the performers. Optimizing human performance is an ongoing condition of a manager's life and requires constant treatment to produce desired results. Approaching performance issues as problems to be fixed or solved is a recipe for frustration and failure.

As in treating any condition, applying a knee-jerk or reactive approach will not produce favorable results. Managers must adopt a proactive method that can be called upon instantaneously and reliably to deal with performance issues.

Unlearning Our Scripts

The generations populating organizations today differ significantly from past generations. Although children in past generations have been imprinted and socialized by parents, family members, church, school, books, and newspapers, the present working generations have had another profound influence in their early years. They have been continually exposed to high intensity bombardment from the visual media. Movies and television, the "electronic babysitter," have played a significant role in programming young people since the 1950s.

The electronic media have the power to touch the senses in a powerful way. However, there are limitations on detailed information and thus content is provided in a condensed manner. Through media filters, people have been programmed on many lessons of life: how to live, how to deal with gender and race relations, how to get along with others, what is right, what is wrong, and so on. In a large sense, our cultural mythology is passed on, generation to generation, through the stories and roles conveyed through the electronic media. Much like the ancient campfires where youth would sit on elders' knees and listen to the stories of the culture, the movie theater and the TV den are today's cultural classrooms.

Through movies and, especially, television—where the programming of values was mainlined into our living rooms—we were provided with models and lessons about what roles worked best for a successful life. Were these models really representative of adult family or work life? Or did these images produce expectations that would never be met? Either way, we were programmed with ideas of what roles in life people should play, and generations have been programmed similarly ever since.

In addition to family issues, a significant lesson learned from story lines and themes in television and movies was how to lead people. We were taught how to take charge, what role the leader played, and what people in charge did to succeed. We watched westerns, detective stories, dramas, and sitcoms that all provided models of what people do when they are in charge. It didn't matter which program we tuned in to; they were all clones, and the leadership message was always the same. The person in charge has been portrayed as the rugged individualist who solves problems that mere mortals can't. Although we have admired the leadership qualities portrayed by the electronic media, there are lessons in these portrayals that don't do us a lot of good today.

Some Life Lessons

Did father really know best? (only until you got married!)

And what about Ozzie Nelson? He didn't have a job, never had any worries (except when they ran out of ice cream), and lived in a wonderful house in a nice neighborhood.

And the Cleaver brothers? Beaver and Wally…no sibling rivalries, no unmanageable spats. Was this reality?

Everything always works out for the best when Bill Cosby is the Dad!

With three crime scene investigations on prime time, we continue to have three males in the dominate leader roles (at least women have advanced from nonactive roles to sidekicks!).

Larry Miller, noted business author, often talks of growing up with the Lone Ranger, whose stereotypical role conveys one of the many cloned leadership messages.. For those who may have watched just one of the Lone Ranger programs or any of the other cloned variations on the theme, you have seen them all. The story line is always the same: there is a problem down on the ranch (or somewhere). The bewildered victims who got themselves into this situation have no ideas or means to solve their own problems. These normal people always seem to represent the bottom of the gene pool. And then, over the dusty prairie, wearing white leotards and a black mask, rides the Lone Ranger. With his super instincts, he always knows that there is a problem down on the ranch. To validate his analysis, he sends his ethnic sidekick, Tonto, into town to investigate. (It is instructive to note that Tonto or his clones on other shows seem to be of minority persuasion and their roles are secondary to the leader and major problem solver.) And sure enough, every week Tonto finds out that there is in fact a problem down on the ranch. And every week Tonto gets his butt kicked finding out.

The rest of the roles are also stereotypes. The rancher is normally the senior citizen who can never figure things out. The rancher usually has a granddaughter who only gets to cook, clean, serve coffee, and ring the dinner triangle. And finally there is the grandson who always seems to be into mischief or causing trouble of some kind. These roles are not productive or contributory, and the messages are clear.

Every week, the Lone Ranger, with his profound leadership skills, figured out the problem, diagnosed who the bad guys were, solved the problem by himself, and put the bad guys in jail. In thirty minutes, the problem was solved,

> *Lone Ranger Leadership*
> *The individualistic, authoritarian leader has all the answers, creating dependency in the followers.*

the day was saved. There was no problem too difficult for the leader.

And at the end of every show, the other players validated their lesser status. There was always a party at the ranch to celebrate their new beginning, and, for some reason, the Lone Ranger slipped away unnoticed. Now how could anyone dressed like that slip away unnoticed? And, to top that, during the time he helped these people with the biggest problem of their lives, no one bothered to ask his name!

Inappropriate Lessons from the Lone Ranger

- ✓ There is always a problem down on the ranch.
- ✓ The people who have the problem are unable to solve it.
- ✓ The leader is the only one skilled at problem solving.
- ✓ Problems are solved within very short time periods.
- ✓ Leadership is an individual, authoritarian role.
- ✓ Males dominate leader roles.

"Who was that masked man?" This is the question asked at the end of every show. And someone speaks out, "Why that was the Lone Ranger!" The room is silent with awe. At this point, you can see the problem created by this type of leadership. The look on the faces of the players when they realize the Lone Ranger is gone is one of despair. They seem to be thinking, "Oh boy, now what? What if we have another problem next week?"

You see, the Lone Ranger never rode into town and conducted ranger classes. The performance of others was never an issue. The powers of leadership, problem solving, and performance were *vested only* in the leader. And the leader took great personal satisfaction from the role. And we all learned vicariously, through observation and reinforcement, the role of the leader and the various roles of the followers.

Today, we see our mythology regarding leadership, management, and "being in charge" replayed again and again. The western heroes have been replaced with new action heroes and comic book heroes. Watch and listen as the lessons of Lone Ranger management are played out on the silver screen and television. Only the names have changed: Spider-Man, Bat-Man, James Bond, The Terminator, Dare-Devil, Dirty Harry, Gandolf, Jason Bourne, Dumbledore, and real people who portray many of the "take charge" leader roles such as Arnold Schwarzenegger, Bruce Willis, Steven Seagal, and Clint Eastwood. Over time, our leader mythology stays the course.

These lessons, while enjoyable and entertaining, are not productive for today's leaders and managers. Consensus building, developing others, joint problem solving, and empowerment are talents that leaders and managers need to master to deal with organizational issues. The reliance on one person to make all the decisions and to formulate all plans is a recipe for failure. Most issues are too complex, the need to change is too commonplace, the demand for real time performance is too routine, and the requirement for speed is too constant.

Leadership Realities

✓ Performance issues are usually conditions, not problems to be solved.

✓ People have the capacity to do well, contribute, and solve their own issues.

✓ Leadership is about developing others, not individualism.

✓ All roles are dignified and have meaning.

The real world that managers face does not resemble the scripted world of the Lone Ranger and his contemporary replacements.

Whether the performance issue is a condition that needs treatment or a problem that can be solved, people have an enormous capacity to solve their own problems and perform on their own two feet in the context of appropriate leadership practices. The true measure of leadership is in the behavior of the followers. As Max DePree, former CEO of Herman Miller Co., wrote,

"The signs of leadership are among the followers: Are they reaching their potential? Are they learning? Are they achieving the desired results? Are they serving? Do they manage change gracefully, and do they manage conflict?"

Success in today's business environment calls for superior performance from every role. New leadership scripts are needed; old scripts must be unlearned. The major obligation that leadership has to the organization is to influence the performance of others. For this reason, a leadership method that focuses on the performance needs of others is critical.

Follower Driven

One constant we have gleaned from observing leadership and assessing organizations is how often managers treat employees with a style or approach that is comfortable to the manager but not to the employees. For example, a manager who is comfortable delegating to others uses delegation as a primary approach, regardless of the employee's ability or confidence regarding the task or assignment delegated. The manager will tend to rationalize this approach as attempts to stretch and challenge the employee. Even though the employee may struggle and his or her confidence may suffer, the leader continues to manage in his or her own most comfortable manner. The manager takes the approach that employees must adapt and "get used to me."

This approach is akin to a doctor prescribing "pink pills" for every ailment he or she comes across, regardless of what is best for the patient. In medicine, this would be mal-practice. What should we call it in management?

**Follow the scenario below and see
if it makes sense.**

Doctor: "What seems to be wrong?"

Patient: "My stomach hurts and my throat is swollen."

Doctor: "I have just the thing for you (going over to a shelf that stores a hundred different bottles of pills). Here, try some of these pink pills."

Patient: "Okay, but will they make me better?"

Doctor: "Don't know for sure. They have worked well for others. And besides, I like them. They are my favorite!"

This "managerial comfort zone" approach to managing people creates a culture in which the relationship between manager and employee is *leader driven*: that is, employees have to adapt constantly to the comfort zone of their managers. In this situation, some employees develop (those whose ability and confidence match up with the manager's comfort zone approach), some stagnate (those whose ability and confidence don't quite match up), and some regress (those whose ability and confidence are significantly out of alignment with the manager's comfort zone approach).

For leadership and performance management to be successful and impact both employee productivity and retention in a positive way, management practices should be *follower driven*. It is the manager that needs the adaptability skills to deal effectively with the various abilities and attitude characteristics that individuals bring to different tasks and assignments. To force the employees to adapt is problematic in that their unique abilities and attitudes are what they are—at any given point in time on any given task. Success requires the manager to be the one who adapts to the performance needs of employees.

Pink Pill

The manager's comfort zone approach to leading people, not adapting to the performance needs of others.

Managers have an obligation to direct performance towards the accomplishment of organizational goals and objectives by inspiring the talents of employees, in order to maximize individual and team performance capabilities. This is an obligation that cannot be done haphazardly. The application of a sound method that allows replication, reliability, and expertise in performance management situations is the responsibility of each manager.

CHAPTER 2

Motivation at Work

"There is so much apathy around here I'm getting to the point where I just don't care anymore!"

—anonymous manager

Beer Bust and Softball

Early in my career, I was assigned to manage an industrial facility that had a reputation for poor performance. My task was to turn the place around. My organization was very helpful: a couple of organizational development specialists were assigned to assist with some interviews during my first two weeks to collect data about the issues at this facility. After the data were formatted into a 200-page report complete with executive overview it was apparent that there were three major problems: (1) lack of employee morale, (2) extremely low productivity, and (3). disrespect for authority.

It was very useful having this two weeks' worth of work condensed for my analysis. However, I also remembered my first day at the facility and what I learned from simple observation. Reading what was written on restroom walls indicated a low level of morale, reviewing the lapse in any preventative maintenance program foretold of poor productivity, and the cynical comments and rudeness from employees hinted at a lack of respect for authority. Nonetheless, a two-week, 200-page report that validated my perceptions was a benefit that no manager could ignore!

At the time, I had had all sorts of supervisory and management training on how to lead and manage people. I knew from seminars and from the popular management books that the job of employee morale fell into the lap of the manager. Over the years, I had seen manager after manager be called upon to raise morale at the first sign of unhappy employees. The popular theme from the books was "happy people are productive people;" the seduction of this phrase was too tempting to resist. My mission was clear: if we were going to be productive, we must begin by building morale. So my challenge unfolded in the typical manner.

With the assistance of one of the organizational development specialists, we had a management team meeting to determine the first steps in building organizational morale.

We brainstormed many ideas, put posters all over the room, sent some ideas to "parking lots" (wherever those lots were), and debated and discussed various approaches for hours.

In the early afternoon, one of my junior managers came up with the idea of having a beer bust and softball game for everyone. Upon hearing his idea, my own motivation and morale began to climb. I love softball and beer. This was a great idea, and one that nobody could possibly argue with. Since I was the leader and had veto power over ideas, I immediately declared this to be our first step. So it was to be, a beer bust and softball game for all.

Of course we had to *order* people to attend, which I now look back on as an interesting morale issue itself. I must have been insane, believing that anyone could *mandate* fun, not to mention mandating high morale at work! In carrying out my plan to

> **A Lesson**
>
> There is only one thing worse than a disgruntled, unmotivated, *sober* employee: a disgruntled, unmotivated, *drunk* employee with a baseball bat!

win people over with my morale boosting day, I learned a leadership lesson that has been with me ever since and has forever shaped my thinking on the issue of employee motivation.

Looking back, I now understand that this morale boosting attempt was nothing more than a bribe. And people know when they are being bribed! Many didn't come to work the next day (hung over perhaps...gosh, should have held it on a Friday!). Morale, productivity, and respect did not improve in any way. And to make matters worse, employees demanded another beer bust and game a couple of months later!

> *Beer Bust & Softball*
>
> *The bribery approach to motivation doesn't work and makes things much worse!*

To be honest, I was angry, angry with the employees at their ungratefulness. I gave them a morale day and they gave me back nothing and demanded another beer bust and game. It wasn't until several months later, failing in every manner to make a positive impact at my new facility, that I began to see the error of my ways. The beginning happened after work one day when one of my mid-level

> **Another Lesson**
>
> *Morale* isn't something that can be bought. The work environment has to provide people with opportunities to succeed, to do their best, to be trusted, to be valued, and to be respected. Then morale and productivity can take place.

managers (who had been there forever) decided it was time for a talk. He told me that I couldn't buy motivation or productivity. He said what the people needed was what had been taken away over the years—involvement, participation, a sense of achievement and contribution, and appropriate decision making and control over tasks and assignments.

I would like to say that the facility was turned around quickly with this insight. However, the destruction of trust and the manipulation that had happened made the process of change require a couple of years to complete. Over time, however, a huge leadership lesson was learned. By giving people their jobs back and creating a work environment that provided meaningful participation and dignity to everyone's job, things began to turn around.

Moments of Insanity

When we look at the traditional carrot-and-stick theory of motivation, we must admit that it does not work well, if at all, once people have reached an adequate subsistence level regarding their needs. Beyond health, food, clothing, and shelter, people tend to be motivated by higher level needs. Management cannot provide people with the respect of others, self-respect, a sense of achievement, or pride. It can only create working conditions that provide opportunities for people to seek these things out for themselves. Why then do we continue to try to bribe or punish our way to superior performance? There is certain insanity present when we attempt to do something with a practice that won't work.

To understand what truly motivates individuals to do their best, to give their discretionary effort, we must acknowledge that many of the past accepted motivational practices are in direct conflict with human nature. In many cases, the application of these practices is akin to digging channels *uphill* to increase the water flow!

For example, a manager identifies performance difficulties with employees. Knowing that the employees know how to perform the tasks in question, the manager assumes a motivation problem and begins to apply motivational techniques in order to improve performance. What to do?*

- Donuts in the morning?
- A Friday pizza party?
- An employee of the month program?
- Letters of recognition?
- Monetary awards?

* Hopefully not a beer bust and softball game.

Recognition is a motivator...

but it lacks impact when respect, trust, personal contribution, and meaningful participation in the work are missing! Perhaps management uses recognition first because it is easier and doesn't require looking in the mirror!

All of these choices assume that people need to be fixed—that there is something wrong with them. Where is the evidence? Where is the test of that theory? There is no evidence or test—only managerial knee-jerk assumptions. Any of the above choices won't work (although the goodies will be accepted by employees), because none of these changes any elements of the work environment.

Let's review the beer bust and softball game scenario to critique these motivational practices. By choosing a beer bust and softball game to solve the morale problem, the unquestioned cause-and-effect determination is made; namely, the cause of low morale was the absence of beer and softball! We can cite for certain that we have never heard employees complain that the cause of poor morale was the lack of beer and softball. However, by applying the prescription (beer and softball) to the situation (low morale), a remedy was used that had no relationship to the cause of the situation! This approach is insane, malpractice indeed!

Understanding cause and effect is the managerial leverage when attempting to manage and inspire superior performance. Jumping to a conclusion based on assumptions about cause and effect will provide the manager with a much worse situation than the one being affected. By using the beer bust and softball game approach, management was allowed to ignore the underlying working conditions and relationships that were in fact (and most often always are) the cause of the poor performance situation at the facility.

Do we really believe that lack of goodies is the reason that people don't give their best effort at work? Do we really believe that recognition and praise for performance can instill pride when people don't *own* the work they do, aren't involved in a meaningful way, don't feel respected and trusted, and don't feel they personally influence the outcomes of their tasks or assignments? Let's stop this insanity and begin to dig deeper to understand the true nature of people's motivation in the workplace.

I Mean You No Harm

Years ago, David Berlo suggested the phrase "I mean you no harm" as advice to management regarding the type of work environment that is conducive to high performance. The phrase came from trainers at Sea World who, when asked how long they swam with new whales in the pool before the training began. replied, "Until the whale knows we mean it no harm." They know that, once whales believe that they are in an environment of no harm, they will relax and perform. This concept seems so fundamental and obvious. Perhaps it is because of this that we so often overlook the signs of harm that work life can communicate to employees.

Now we know that reality prevents managers from "swimming" with their employees before job responsibilities begin. However, managers can commit to removing the harmful elements of work life so that fear, intimidation, and

I Mean You No Harm	
Trust	*Dignity*
Respect	*Fairness*
Equity	*Sincerity*

overt stress are eliminated. Managers can begin to build relationships with employees that are grounded in trust, respect, fairness, equity, dignity, and sincerity. Regardless of how many goodies management provides to motivate or reward people, these treats fall flat without an environment of no harm. No amount of money (although gladly accepted) can make up for a work environment that lacks the necessary manager-employee relationship qualities. And beer busts only serve to accelerate the blatant complaining about the poor quality of the workplace.

Managers need to adopt an approach to managing people that says, "I mean you no harm.". This is the foundation for motivation and desire at work. The manager's creed should be to never do personally anything that will destroy trust, suggest favoritism, show discrimination or disrespect to people or their jobs, or communicate insincerity.

The Law of the Hog

There are consequences for neglecting the work environment and the performance and motivational issues necessary for meaningful participation. Years ago, a friend named Kerry Patterson wrote an article entitled "The Law of the Hog." While he was conducting interviews during a consulting contract with a lumber company, evidence of employee mistreatment, both physical and verbal, came to light. The employees, working for a company in a remote location in an environment sort of like a company-owned town, were apathetic about their situation, realizing that they had no other employment choices. However, during one interview with a 20-year employee on the mill floor, information was shared which shed more light on the intolerable leadership situation.

> **The Law of the Hog**
>
> *Predictable employee behavior as a result of mistreatment and nonparticipation.*

This employee said the way the employees got back at management was to "feed the hog." Now the hog was a big piece of machinery, with large sharp teeth, that ground scrap lumber into sawdust. (Visions of supervisors being thrown into the hog appeared.)

The employees would find ways to get good raw product into the hog when supervisors weren't looking. Sometimes there was competition among employees, with the winner (the one who got the most good lumber into the hog) treated to beer by other employees at the local saloon after work. Doesn't this seem like performance management—the most lumber into the hog (goals and objectives), who got the most in the hog (measurement), and beer for the winner (reward for outstanding performance)?

When you think about it, every organization has a hog. Shrinkage, organizational sabotage, stealing, and absenteeism are forms of the hog. Malicious compliance, doing only what you are told to do—nothing more nothing less—is a form of the hog. Vicious compliance, doing exactly what you are told, with enthusiasm—when you know it will fail—is a form of the hog. And the hardest one to measure— poor attitude with customers—is another form of hog behavior. The degree to which the hog gets fed in organizations is a result of the quality of leadership and management practices.

The Hog
✓ Organizational sabotage
✓ Stealing
✓ Shrinkage
✓ Malicious compliance
✓ Vicious compliance
✓ Poor attitude with customers
✓ Absenteeism
✓ Quit and stay
✓ Quit and leave

Patterson's article identified the hog as a metaphor for predictable behavior when people feel mistreated, disenfranchised, and nonparticipating. Because of the predictable nature of people under these circumstances, it is an organizational law. Fail to attend to the performance needs and meaningful participation of others and be prepared to face the hog.

Productive People Are Happy People!

Beer busts and softball games don't motivate people to do good work. Employee of the month programs raise more cynicism than productivity. The hog gets fed in spite of monetary bonuses or profit sharing. The challenge is clear: motivation to perform comes from *within*, and that motivation won't be bought with extrinsic and material lures. And if there is a bribe involved, the unintended consequences are profound. Bob Nelson, noted author and expert on rewards and recognition refers to the bribery technique for motivation as "wreck ignition." We concur!

The motivation to perform comes from a work environment that allows people to be productive, to achieve, and to participate in a meaningful manner. The research, both empirical and face-valid, has long supported this notion. For example, Fredric Herzberg illustrated the difference between what things turned people off (dissatisfiers) and what things turned people on (satisfiers) in the work environment. His landmark work indicated that the absence of dissatisfiers did not lead to satisfaction and motivation, only resulting in people being "not dissatisfied." His research indicated that people would be dissatisfied (unmotivated) when issues such as pay, status, policies, working conditions, and interpersonal relations were in question. However, he noted that performance motivation (satisfaction) comes only with the presence of the ability to achieve, challenging work, increased responsibility, opportunities for growth and development, and recognition for accomplishment. A critical conclusion can be drawn: happy people are not necessarily productive, but productive people are happy.

Indicators for Employee Productivity and Retention

✓ Clear performance expectations

✓ Materials and equipment to do the work right

✓ The opportunity to do what I do best

✓ My supervisor, or someone at work, seems to care about me as a person.

✓ My opinions count.

✓ In the last seven days, I have received recognition for good work.

✓ There is someone at work who encourages my development.

Herzberg's work was validated later by Lawrence Lindahl. When Lindahl posed the question to managers about what they believed motivated employees at work, the managers responded with issues of pay, bonuses, benefits, time off, and such. When Lindhal posed the same question to workers themselves, the responses were much different. Workers responded with issues such as making a difference, responsibility, challenging work, achievement, and recognition. Again, the message is clear: the road to happiness at work is through productivity and performance.

Recently, the Gallup organization cites key indicators that lead to employee productivity and employee retention. These indicators are all related to performance issues and the means for employees to do good work and contribute. There is nothing in the Gallup research that validates extrinsic motivation techniques as the leverage for superior performance, productivity, and retention.

In the face of years of research, you may wonder why we continue to ignore what we know to be true. Perhaps it is because many books and seminars still put forth axioms that lead us to believe that the road to superior performance is through morale lifting programs. Perhaps it is because it is easier. Focusing on building a performance environment where people's contributions make a difference, where people have the conditions that allow them to be their best, and where employee involvement is routine requires attentive leadership that takes time, patience, and practice. It is much easier to simply throw a party!

So, Beware the Seduction

Let's be clear, there is nothing wrong with a beer bust and softball game; it just doesn't motivate people to perform well. Why? It's ineffective because its absence is not the reason that motivation to perform is lacking. When a motivating environment is created, people enjoy a party or get together, of course, but as a "thank-you" or a "breather." However, when the party is used to get something from employees, it not only fail to work, but it usually backfires, making things worse..

There is nothing wrong with praise, recognition, and rewards; they just don't motivate when they are used to get something in return (i.e., strings attached). When people are contributing and productive, then praise, recognition, and rewards that are used as a sincere thank-you and a show of appreciation for good work already performed are welcomed. The trick is not to confuse the parties, praise, recognition, and rewards with the practices that lead to the type of performance that *deserves* parties, praise, recognition, and rewards.

The confusion can lead to work conditions that not only do not improve performance results, but make matters worse. Consider employee-of-the-month programs. Our experience with employee assessments indicates that these programs not only fail to do what they are intended, but create undesirable emotions in the workplace. The following example serves to illustrate our point.

While checking into a hotel on a business trip, we noticed twelve pictures (employees of the month) in a circle on the perimeter of a nice mahogany plaque behind the front desk. We consider these situations as research opportunities; the dialogue with the young lady who checked us in went as follows:

Motioning to the plaque behind her, *"Is that your company recognition program?"*

Turning and looking and then responding with little emotion, *"Oh that, yea."*

Noticing that all twelve pictures on the plaque were different, *"I wonder if you would mind if I asked a question?"*

"Sure."

"Can you tell me why no employee has his or her picture up on the plaque more than once?"

Looking at us as if we had just arrived on the planet, *"Well, you can't win it more than once."*

Asking in a curious manner, *"You mean no matter how well you perform, you can't win it more than once?"*

Responding as if we were totally clueless, *"Sir, what makes you think this (pointing at the plaque) has anything to do with performance?"*

Still curious, *"Well, another question then…that picture in the middle of the twelve, the employee of the year…you would think to win employee of the year you would have to be good enough to have won employee of the month in at least one month!"*

Shaking her head, *"Probably just his turn."*

And still pursuing obvious answers, *"One last question…how do you win these awards?"*

With a blank expression, *"I really have no idea."*

Let's analyze this conversation. Management creates a program, employee of the month, to single out and recognize outstanding performance. The people who receive the reward don't believe the award has anything to do with performance. The outstanding employee of the year didn't perform well enough to win employee of the month in any one month. And people don't know what the criteria for winning the award might be. This is not a recognition program—it a program for creating cynicism! Again, insanity rules the day.

> **Your Recognition Programs**
>
> ✓ Can people win more than once?
>
> ✓ Does it recognize those who help and assist?
>
> ✓ Do people know the criteria for winning?
>
> ✓ Is it a thank-you or a bribe?
>
> ✓ Does it foster cooperation or competition?
>
> ✓ Is the winner's circle restricted to a population of more than one?

Now you might be thinking that we merely ran into a disgruntled employee. Well, this lady had a great attitude and her performance at the front desk was above average. But really, to rationalize this situation by focusing on the employee's reaction is to deny the morass of evidence regarding programs of this type. Look around and see all the plaques that have outdated pictures (the program died on the vine) or that have not been kept current. Talk to employees when you run into these programs and elicit their reactions. No, this is the norm; it is not unusual.

Not only that, organizational leaders are constantly calling for more teamwork and cooperation between employees. Then they create recognition programs that single out employees for recognition. Do we really believe that performance by individuals in an organization is done without the help and assistance of others? Do we really believe that we have the kind of metrics that allow us to determine who is best in most jobs in any one month, much less for any one year? Why do we cry out for cooperation and then continually create programs that celebrate individual performance at the expense of others, restrict the winners' circle to one, and influence employees to compete against each other for limited recognition? Do we really believe this creates the kind of emotions and behaviors that lead to superior, team-oriented performance?

> ### Whale of the Month
> *Recognition programs that create cynicism and destructive competition and are not focused on performance.*

At Sea World, there is no Whale-of-the-Month program. The conditions are set up for each whale to perform at his or her best. They do. Each whale understands what is expected, the materials and equipment are provided so each whale can perform at his or her best, instances of recognition given for good work are always much less than seven days apart, and there are trainers who truly care about the whales. There is enough fish, squid, and recognition for every whale, and it is well *earned*.

Organizational performance is the measure of leadership. Within ethical and legal boundaries, managers and supervisors are tested on how well they inspire and influence the performance of their direct reports. In looking at managerial ability, the test is clear. Can employees perform well, stand on own two feet, achieve, contribute, and make a difference? Is managerial recognition of employee performance based on employee accomplishment, not a bribe for future performance? To create a motivating performance environment,

> ### A Leadership Method That Influences
> ✓ Superior performance
> ✓ Employee initiative
> ✓ Individual responsibility
> ✓ Achievement
> ✓ Contribution
> ✓ Accomplishment
> ✓ Growth and development

managers need a leadership method that influences individual responsibility, superior performance, and meaningful contribution.

CHAPTER 3

Performance Expectations

"I always wanted to be somebody. I now wish I had been a little more specific."

—Lily Tomlin,
The Search for Signs of Intelligent Life in the Universe.

The First Question: Are Performance Expectations Clear?

Using the *Performance Advantage Method* requires asking a series of questions to get performance information and then taking appropriate leadership action depending on your answers. So let's start at the beginning: Are performance expectations clear?

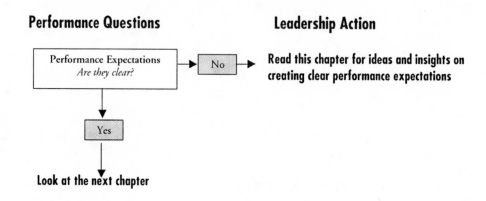

Performance Questions

Leadership Action

Performance Expectations
Are they clear? → No → **Read this chapter for ideas and insights on creating clear performance expectations**

Yes

Look at the next chapter

Five on Five

Years ago, we embarked on a project to determine how well managers were communicating their performance expectations to their direct reports. After several years of conducting management seminars and organizational development interventions, our conclusion was that a major cause of poor or unacceptable performance was the lack of clarity about (1) what performance was expected, (2) what standard of performance was expected, and (3) how performance was to be measured. Most managers we talked with, then and since, have prided themselves on their ability to set goals and objectives. All gave themselves credit for being clear with employees about what was expected at work. This notwithstanding, these same managers talked about the myriad of difficulties they had getting good performance on a routine basis.

We began to conduct a very simple experiment. We asked each manager to write down the name of a particular employee with whom he or she was having performance difficulties. We then asked the manager to write down the five critical performance expectations (goals and objectives) for which the employee was responsible. We also asked the manager to prioritize these five expectations in the order of importance to the organizational goals.

Once we had the manager's list of five expectations, we then asked the employee in question to list the five critical performance expectations for which he or she was responsible. We asked the employee to prioritize these five expectations as he or she believed the manager would.

Over the course of 10 years, we conducted this process with over 2,000 mangers and supervisors. Our results were striking. The average number of expectations that showed up on both the manager list and the employee list was just a little over two expectations! And the prioritization that was possible with only two similar expectations was almost always different. If employees are focused on issues that the manager isn't, performance difficulties are predictable. Without alignment on performance expectations, managerial practices such as measurement, feedback, and recognition are moot. The feedback we received after conducting this process with managers was that they experienced considerable performance improvement just by getting the two parties focused on the same expectations.

> *Five on Five*
>
> *The process of manager/employee performance expectation alignment*

Is it any wonder that a critical indicator of employee productivity and employee retention according to much of the research including the recent Gallup research is "knowledge of what is expected of me at work." It's demoralizing to find out that what you've been working hard at isn't what you should have been focusing on. This realization negatively impacts the human spirit. The manager's first responsibility in performance management is to provide clarity regarding performance expectations.

What Does Good Performance Look Like?

Another lament we often heard from employees was how often they felt in the dark regarding how well they were performing. When we asked about their performance appraisal or performance evaluation process, we got what we know to be true of many of those methods: they don't provide very good feedback on how well people are doing because the category that people are put in is either predetermined or performance is generalized into ambiguous characteristics that provide little, if any, real measure of performance.

When No News Is Good News

If the only time you hear from the boss is when performance is poor, the workplace conversation you want to avoid is the one with the boss!

So we began to ask employees the question, "How do you know when you are doing a good job?" The responses carried a central theme, "No news is good news." The absence of criticism or rebuke was the main indicator that work was well done. When we asked employees how they knew they were performing poorly, they responded rapidly, "Oh, you hear quickly about that!" Now you might consider that this indicates a lack of positive feedback or praise in the work environment, and you would be correct. However, there is a deeper issue here than the lack of recognition for doing a good job.

Carrying the "five on five" process one step further, we asked managers to write down for the five critical performance expectations what level of performance was considered outstanding and what level was considered acceptable (acknowledging that below the acceptable level was unacceptable performance). We asked the employees (with their new lists that were aligned with the managers' lists) to do the same. Again the results were mind-boggling.

On each index, outstanding performance and acceptable performance, there was normally a 60 to 70 percent difference regarding agreement on performance levels. When we asked each party to list how each performance expectation was to be measured, we again found the normative differences in the 60 to 70 percent range, with most employees stating that they didn't know how the manager measured performance.

If managers don't have clarity on what good performance looks like, they have a tendency to react to poor performance when it happens and to take acceptable performance for granted. Their reactions to performance take place only when performance drops to a level that causes obvious and visible problems. No amount of attention to recognize and praise employees will make up for this dilemma. And when employees are not clear on the standards regarding outstanding and acceptable performance or aware of how their performance is to be measured, they are left *dependent* on the manager to provide performance feedback. They can't take personal responsibility for performance improvement and self-govern their own performance.

Attention Is All There Is

In Search of Excellence author, Tom Peters, once said that if you want to know what employees think is important to their boss and what issues employees would focus on during their time at work, just look at the boss's calendar. Where does the boss spend his or her time? What issues take up the bulk of the boss's time? What are the agenda items during the boss's meetings? In short, where the boss spends time and what the boss pays attention to constitutes what employees will think is important.

We learned this lesson about the impact of behavior and the power of behavior over words in kindergarten. Remember *Simon Says*? The lesson was clear. As adults, we have created clichés to reinforce that message, "Walk your talk."

So often we run into situations where managers will state what they expect and then allow their behavior to undermine their very words. At best, this creates confusion for employees. At worst, it shifts the focus on what is expected. Both of these situations

> **Behavior, Not Words**
>
> Provides clarity regarding performance expectations, goals, and objectives

are undesirable. Managers must align their behavior with the expectations they have for followers. Managers must be enthusiastic and act in ways that communicate the importance of the expectations they say they want. If managers want employees to pay attention to certain things, then the managers must put their attention there also.

To paraphrase Emerson,

> *"Your behavior thunders so loudly your words will not be heard!"*

Accountability and Expectations

Before managers set performance expectations, they must be committed to hold people accountable. Without the will to enforce the expectations they place on employees, managers will sabotage the expectations and goal setting process. We have seen many seminars and writings on goal and objective setting that fail to address the issue of accountability. This is interesting in that the accountability process of a manager does much more to create *clarity* regarding goals and expectations than does the goal setting process.

Consider the following example: speed limits on the interstate. Let's say the speed limit is 65 miles per hour. The state government has decided on this speed as safe and has provided goal clarity by posting signs along the highway proclaiming 65 mph as the performance expectation for drivers. There is no ambiguity regarding the expectation printed on the sign post. So, given such clarity, everyone performs at this expectation, right? Hardly!

People test the *tolerance* for this stated expectation and the *real* speed limit—and thus the perceived expectation—is whatever is tolerated. Let's just say that staying under 75 mph is tolerated. After driving with the normal flow at about 74 mph for months, when drivers gets ticketed for going the speed that has been tolerated over time, they feel it is unfair due to the inconsistency of accountability. The authority figure (management) is seen as the problem!

Following this example further, let's say you buy in and you put forth an effort to drive safely at the posted speed limit. You see other drivers speeding, doing fast lane changes when passing others, and basically not abiding by what is expected. For many, their first thought is, "Where is a cop when you need one? I hope they get caught."

Now consider the same scenario but you also observe a highway patrol officer who sees this speeding driver. The highway patrol officer does nothing. At this point, who are you mad at now? Again, for many, anger shifts to the officer for not doing his or her job. This scenario is revisited in the workplace routinely. People who buy in to the objectives of the organization work side by side with a person who doesn't care, who does

Accountability Failure Results in
✓ Redefinition of expectations
✓ Performance adjusts to the tolerance level.
✓ Frustration and anger with management
✓ Good people quit and leave.
✓ Some quit and stay.

poor work, and who ignores the required performance expectations. When the manager does nothing, frustration, cynicism, and anger set in. The stated performance expectations are questioned, and future performance adjusts to the tolerance level that management decides to enforce. Consistent managerial acts of no accountability dumb down the organizational performance level to the lowest common denominator.

> ### 65 mph Speed Limit
> *Accountability creates consistent clarity for performance expectations and is an important element of a motivating work environment.*

Performance expectations and goal clarity are the result of consistent and reliable accountability. Managerial accountability sends the message that what is said is what is really meant. Accountability provides integrity to expectations. When managers fail to provide consistent accountability for the expectations they have set, performance problems are predictable. Initially, people want those who abuse expectations and performance standards to be held accountable for their actions. People look to those "in charge" to take some initiative and to correct performance problems. When poor performance is not addressed, people lose their enthusiasm and go with the flow. Performance expectations lose their clarity, and performance continues to suffer.

As a side note, this issue of accountability is strongly related to motivation at work. Time and time again, research shows that the number one thing that frustrates and demotivates people during working hours is having to work side by side with someone who doesn't care or doesn't carry his or her weight and having management tolerate this action.

Management does a service to high performing and caring employees by holding poor performers accountable and demanding improvement. Failure to do so is an injustice to good performers and communicates that their efforts are not valued. Nothing will contaminate a performance environment as much as high tolerance for poor performance. A motivating work environment cannot be achieved without a consistent and reliable accountability process on performance expectations.

The Power of Purpose

All performance expectations should connect with both the mission of the organization and the human impact those expectations affect. This gives meaning and purpose to the performance activities people engage in. When the connection is clear and the alignment is made between performance expectations and some higher purpose, people tend to bring more to the workplace than just the need to trade time for money.

People need to know their work makes a difference.

✓ The guest's stay is more enjoyable as a result of the talent of the housekeeper.

✓ The shopping experience is delightful due to the attentiveness and knowledge of the sales person.

✓ A trip to the dentist is affected by the attention to detail in patient scheduling.

✓ Everyone notices cleanliness even though they may not comment on it, and it takes talent to keep things noticeably clean.

✓ Accurate invoicing avoids the trouble of customers using their spare time to resolve problems.

Performance makes a difference everywhere, and people who perform are entitled to know about the difference their work makes!

And we must be suspicious of the financial purposes that managers utilize to motivate employee performance. Although financial objectives are important and making money is critical to organizational health and growth, they alone will not satisfy the motivational and inspirational needs of employees. Rarely is anyone other than senior executives really moved by a return to shareholder investment. Profit margins are useful to know about, but they are hardly inspirational, other than for a moment's "rah-rah." Acquisitions and mergers are exciting for only a few individuals while causing concern and apprehension in many others. Financial issues rarely change significantly for the majority of employees when organizational performance improves. And even when it does, the effect is short lived because a new baseline is established. Mission statements are interesting to management but often very abstract when used to inspire the performance of most employees.

Many managers have forgotten how to inspire others. They have been consumed and seduced by our knowledge and love for using techniques on others to get desired performance. Although many of these techniques seem to contain managerial magic and are easy to use, managers do not acknowledge their failure to inspire the soul of the average worker. The result is a management population that goes about "doing things" to employees while simultaneously employees don't much like things being done to them! This cycle of insanity is painfully present in many organizations.

Russ Linden, author of *Working Across Boundaries,* cites an application of connecting people's work with a higher purpose. He refers to the process as "line of sight." He defines *line of sight* as connecting what each individual employee does to its ultimate impact on another human being. Linden cites an example from the

> ## Line of Sight
> *Connecting what each individual employee does to its ultimate impact on another human being*

Department of Motor Vehicles (DMV) in a particular state where one department was responsible for processing Form 47. When asked how they knew they were doing a good job, they replied, "If there is less than a six-week backlog, no one comes in and yells at us." This relevance and importance of a person's work activities is hardly inspiring, and it makes performance very ambiguous

However, the highway patrol in this state understands the vital importance of Form 47, which is the notification that someone has received three DUIs and allows patrolmen to take that person off the road immediately. Not only that, when the new director of the DMV had the opportunity to meet the head of Mothers Against Drunk Drivers (MADD) for that state, he gained yet another perspective. During a discussion, when she became aware that there was a performance problem with the Form 47 group, she said something to this effect, "My god, don't you realize how important Form 47 is? My son would be alive today if the highway patrol had earlier access to Form 47."

The new director invited both the highway patrol and the head of MADD for the state to come talk to his Form 47 group. The result was that the processing time for Form 47 went from six weeks to three days! This example illustrates that every piece of work has some impact on the human experience: either affecting a customer, a supplier, a constituent, or other co-workers. This is the process of "connecting the dots" that must take place to provide clarity to performance expectations beyond what people do and how they will be measured.

For many, connecting performance expectations to a purpose beyond financial success or the acquisition of good performance marks is enough. The salary, wage, and benefit issues have been settled and

> ## Cause Worthy of Commitment
> *Performance expectations connected to a purpose beyond financial success and performance appraisal*

are *givens.* Good marks for good performance represent an *earned* result of employee efforts. Promotions come and go...there are not always enough openings and opportunities. However, all good performance has a positive impact on someone and something. And good performance results from the talents of the employee. Knowledge of how performance

- makes a difference to others,
- serves a higher purpose than financial results,
- builds the character and culture of a company, and
- contributes to the organizational mission

gives people a cause worthy of their commitment and inspires them beyond compliance performance. So much can be gained with so little effort from this process that it is a wonder why it is so overlooked.

I Don't Know. I Just Work Here.

How often do we hear the refrain, "I don't know. I just work here." as an answer to questions of why work is done the way it is. The other fallback is the employee retort "It's the policy." Neither answer addresses the "why" question' and neither answer shows any indication that the employees understand why they do things the way they do. How can people get excited about doing things when they don't understand the reasons for doing them the way they are asked? How embarrassed will people be when they have to respond to questions with these unsatisfactory answers? It is predictable that, in such situations, employees will always be on the defensive with customers and other employees, eventually feel frustrated, and perform in a less than satisfactory manner.

> *I Don't Know. I Just Work Here.*
>
> *Employees who don't know why things are done they way they are leave others frustrated and dissatisfied with their performance.*

Clarity concerning why employees must do things a certain way is just as important as clarity about what they are supposed to do. Without understanding the reasons, employees can't do the following:

- Explain to customers the reasons that things are done certain ways, thus leaving customers frustrated and dissatisfied.
- Explain to other employees the reasons for doing things, thus creating more friction and conflict within the organization.

- Bring the necessary level of enthusiasm to the performance of their jobs.

The apathetic, low enthusiastic approach that many employees bring to their jobs can be substantially eliminated by providing clear performance expectations and understanding *why* the expectations are necessary—why they are asked to do things a certain way.

Focus on Outcomes

By clarifying performance expectations in the form of outcomes, managers will save time and effort in their performance management activities and influence higher levels of achievement. The needless process of defining performance expectations in terms of tasks, activities, and duties creates more performance management headaches than we realize.

Outcomes are what are important to the organization, the manager, and the employee. Tasks, activities, and duties are irrelevant if their accomplishment does not result in desirable outcomes. Why bother creating performance expectations around inputs (means) when their accomplishment is inherent in the outcome? Although managers might want to measure the performance of the *quality* of tasks, activities, and duties that lead to outcomes for the purpose of teaching and coaching, measuring their *quantity* is unnecessary because the outcome measure is the valid yardstick of performance. Precious time is wasted and other unintended consequences result from a means-ends reversal when managers create clear performance outcomes.

> ### One Size Fits One
> *Acknowledgment of the individual personalities and talents of employees provides them with the opportunity to maximize their individual potential. Focusing on the outcomes, not the means promotes personal talent.*

Focusing performance expectations on outcomes also helps managers avoid the temptation to control the methods that employees use to maximize their talents and to have employees conform to the manager's way of doing things. By allowing leeway on the means and methods of performance, managers take advantage of the individual personalities, behavior characteristics, and talents of individual employees. Standardizing the outcomes and creating high performance standards means not having to standardize and focus on the means of achievement, thereby allowing for the true talents of individuals to emerge.

All performance can be turned into outcome expectations. Some performance issues might require some deeper thinking, but it can be done. A file clerk's performance expectations should not be focused on the task of filing but on the outcome of fast and accurate retrieval of information. A sales person's performance expectations are not centered on relationship building, product knowledge, handling objections, or attention to detail (all important competencies to be developed) but on the outcome of sales volume. A customer service worker is not expected to perform rigid recipes or scripts while serving customers but to make the customer's experience worthy of repeat business. The effort that goes into this process will provide managers with a high return on investment regarding their performance management time and activities.

There is no one best way to perform to achieve desired results. Unique and individual characteristics regarding people's talents and skills are prerequisite ingredients that make up superior performance. Effective managers won't require

> **The Nervous Boss**
>
> A major cause of managerial anxiety is realizing that your people will not do things the way you would. And nothing will change that!

similar execution of performance; they will simply demand that everyone arrive at the same destination.

Behavioral Values

For many managers, focusing performance expectations on outcomes and allowing deviation and leeway in the methods of performance are unthinkable. We often hear comments such as these: "They'll cut corners," "We're governed by regulations and people can't do it their way," "You just open the door for unethical or unlawful behavior." Although the concern is real, the answer does not lie in micromanaging every method of performance.

In 1914, before he hired the company's first employee, Tom Watson, Sr., of IBM wrote the following three operating core values for his company: "One, the individual must be respected. Two, the customer must be given the best possible service. Three, excellence and superior performance must be pursued."

He wanted his employees to understand the kind of company he intended to build. Most importantly, he wanted them to understand the boundaries within which each employee's performance must operate. He also wanted them to know that, if they demonstrated a set of values incompatible with his, they would be fired! His son and other leaders who followed at IBM all believe that their success was built on these values. We still talk with "old-timers" at IBM and observe them getting misty eyed when reflecting on the days when those values were the mainstay of their organization.

At American Honda, we found a similar commitment to company values. Before we could do a presentation for a division of American Honda, we were sent a copy of Honda's core values and told that we could not work for Honda—even for two hours—without clearly understanding and agreeing to work within their value system. These values provided the behavioral boundaries for the development and delivery of our presentation. Within the boundaries of these values, we had all the autonomy and leeway we needed to be successful.

This is the answer to a concern about outcome-based performance expectations: creating behavioral core values that place limitations on individual and group action regarding how they perform their responsibilities. Outcome-based performance expectations can be utilized with confidence when core values are used to restrict the type of behavior that will jeopardize the organization or its members.

> ### *Freedom, Not License*
> *This is the title of A.S. Neill's best-selling book. Its thesis is that everyone, including children, can learn to be self-disciplined and responsible only by gaining freedom, not being restricted. Neill, however, is quick to point out that freedom does not mean you can do absolutely whatever you like. There are boundaries. And, if the boundaries are examined regularly to ensure appropriate-ness and a lot of breathing room, people will act responsibly.*

Consider the following sample list of core values:

- Act with integrity and honesty in all actions.
- Treat every individual with dignity and respect.
- Continuously attempt to improve everything we do.
- Protect the long-term financial health of the company.
- If you can't do it safely, legally, or ethically, don't do it!

A set of core behavioral values such as these need not exist only at the organizational level. Managers can customize the message of the organizational values. or they can create their own in the absence of organizational values for application within their own division, department, or work group. These values serve as notice to all regarding the behaviors that are desired and valued by the organization, and they provide guidelines to employees about *how* to act. Additionally, they also guide individual decision making and put limitations on the manner and method that employees use to achieve performance results.

Define the Playing Field	Core behavioral values *define the playing field*—the performance arena—for each

Define the Playing Field

Create behavioral values that dictate "how" employees perform their duties.

Core behavioral values *define the playing field*—the performance arena—for each employee. Within this playing field, employees can use their individual talents and diverse methods to achieve results. This then allows performance expectations to be focused on outcomes without encumbering employees with a "one size fits all" approach to how to do their job.

Defining the playing field means clarifying for employees what can be done. as well as setting limits. It has been our experience that most attempts at pushing responsibility and initiative into the employee's arena have failed because management has not created a clearly defined playing field on which the frontline can effectively manage risk. Only when management fulfills its responsibilities to take the ambiguity out of performance expectations and provide boundaries that define the limits of employee action will employees be willing to take the risks associated with their performance responsibilities. When the playing field is clearly understood, initiative, performance, and risks are infinitely more manageable.

Leadership Action

When *performance expectations* are not clear, the leadership action should be to "*ESTABLISH*" what is needed. Leadership actions such as training, teaching, supporting, encouraging, reprimands, or discipline will not help the performance situation when unclear performance expectations are the causal element.

Performance Question   ## Leadership Action

To *ESTABLISH* performance expectations and remove ambiguity and confusion regarding what is expected,

- Spell out areas of responsibility in outcome-based terms.*

- Spell out performance standards, i.e., the accepted performance levels.

- Spell out methods of performance measurement.

- Provide clarity around timelines (how often measured; due dates).

- Connect performance to mission and purpose, the "So what?" factor.

- Illustrate how the performance issue affects other people, i.e., the human condition.

- Ensure understanding of consequences of poor performance.

- Ensure that employees understand the context and relevance (reasons for importance) of the work they are expected to perform.

- Make clear the consequences to the organization if performance failures or missed deadlines occur.

Organizational performance is work that leads to any outcome that is deemed valuable to the success of the organization. This is what people are paid to do. This is what managers are responsible for influencing. Remember, the number one managerial obligation to the enterprise is to inspire people to perform at their best.

---

* Research indicates that there is substantially more clarity, less ambiguity, and greater influencing impact when performance expectations are *written* down and not left to memory.

CHAPTER 4

Ability Deficiencies?

"The whole art of teaching is only the art of awakening the natural curiosity of young minds for the purpose of satisfying it afterward."

—Anatole France

The second question using the *Performance Advantage Method* centers on the employees' *ability* to perform the task or activity in question.

Performance Questions   **Leadership Action**

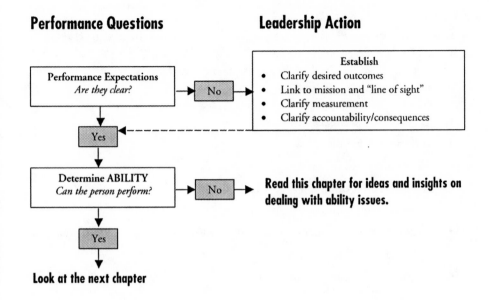

Look at the next chapter

Eligibility and Suitability

Performance success in jobs requires a combination of two distinctly different types of core competencies: technical and behavioral. These two competencies can be labeled *eligibility* and *suitability*.

Eligibility =	"can do"
Suitability =	"will do"

Eligibility determines whether a person *can* do the performance requirements within a particular job. Generally speaking, eligibility consists of the following:

- Specific skill
- Previous work experience
- Training
- Education

These technical competencies (eligibility factors) are far more easily measured than behavioral ones. They are more quantifiable and can generally be observed, tested, and verified.

Suitability determines whether a person *will* do the performance requirements of a particular job. *Does he or she posses the behavioral tendencies for the job and will he or she fit in and play well with others?* Generally, suitability consists of the following behavioral competencies:

- Leadership and decision-making skills
- Interpersonal skills
- Motivation and initiative
- Attitudinal requirements
- Personal honesty, values, and ethics
- Task preferences, personal interests, and work environment preferences
- Personality balance
- Culture and organizational compatibility

Suitability

Behavioral preferences and willingness to "play well with others" and perform job tasks well make a person a fit for the job and organization.

To leverage high performance in any organization, jobs must be analyzed to determine the correlation between superior performance and (1) eligibility requirements for that particular job and (2) suitability requirements for that particular job.. Once these have been accomplished, people can be assessed to determine both eligibility and suitability the factors that predict performance success. This process is ideal; we find more organizations moving in this direction as the cost of poor performance through poor selection, poor promotions, and poor succession planning are profound.

However, whether an organization follows this or a similar process, or whether traditional forms of hiring, assigning, and promoting are followed, the critical component of performance management is the manager's ability to influence and coach people to perform at desired performance standards. Once performance expectations are established, we next deal with the performance issues that result from ability deficiencies.

What Is Ability?

For the purposes of performance management, we define *ability* as the degree of

- knowledge,
- past experience, and
- applied skill

a person brings to bear on a specific task or activity. Another aspect of ability is that it is not a relevant personal label to apply to others. Ability is not a characteristic that reflects the person, but a characteristic that correlates to how well a person can do something in particular. Thus it is important for managers to look at a specific job function, task, activity, or area of responsibility when determining employee ability to perform.

> **Determining Ability**
>
> If the employee's *life* depended upon performing at the desired standard, could he or she do it?
>
> - No = Ability deficiency
> - Yes = Attitude issue

Ability must be considered with respect to a standard of performance for a specific performance issue. A person might have swung and hit a pitched baseball, now and then, but can't hit the ball often enough to be productive in playing the game of baseball. A person might balance the accounting books every so often but can't consistently keep the books balanced. In both of those cases, an ability deficiency is present because the performance is not up to the desired standard.

$$\text{Ability} = \frac{\textbf{Knowledge, Past Experiences, Applied Skill}}{\textbf{Desired Standard of Performance}}$$

The Potential/Capability Trap

A difficulty in performance management that many managers face is when they associate ability with potential or capability. We can gauge a person's potential and capability by reviewing his or her educational background, past work experiences, and past performance record as indications of future achievement.

However, until a person meets desired performance criteria in any specific performance area, ability is absent: only potential/capability is present.

A trap in performance management that many managers fall into is to attempt to manage and influence people at the level of performance at which managers believe they could or should be (potential) or at which they used to be (past performance results: capability). Performance management leverage results from managing and influencing people where they are: at present performance results (ability level). Managers who deal with performance issues in present terms are much more effective and get better results than those who live in the past or in the future!

What About Attitude?

We sometimes consider the ability level of people for specific performance areas before dealing with the attitudinal characteristics of people for the following reasons:

- When a person lacks ability, the lack of confidence to perform is affected mostly by providing that person with training and practice that will raise the ability level, not by merely encouraging and supporting them in their efforts to do better.

- Lack of desire or motivation to perform can be the result of low ability level. Providing the means to raise the ability level is an appropriate action, whereas reprimand, lecture, or consequences are not.

Results of reprimand or punishment for *ability deficiencies*
• Damage personal relationships
• Erode motivation
• Put at risk improved productivity and performance

When the attitudinal issues result from the lack of ability, improving that ability is the only effective treatment to alter the performer's confidence and motivation. Only after people have the ability can their managers accurately diagnose and pinpoint other causes for attitudinal issues with a negative effect on performance outcomes. Failure to assess attitudinal *causes* accurately can lead to damaging consequences.

We have encountered many situations in which employees have been reprimanded, disciplined, or punished for poor performance by managers who have determined the cause of the poor performance to be a poor attitude towards the job. In many of these situations, the diagnosis of the poor attitude was incomplete; there was an ability deficiency present as well. No amount of threats or punishment will affect an ability issue. However, the relationship between the manager and employee will surely be affected negatively, resulting in the employee either quitting and leaving or quitting and staying. Both of these outcomes are unfortunate for the organization, the manager, and the employee.

Another important issue regarding the need to determine ability deficiencies dealing with attitudinal issues that affect performance is culture. Western culture and, to an even greater extent, most corporate

> Being known for *"not knowing how"* to do things is not desirable within organizations. Thus, people readily *mask* ability deficiencies!

and organizational cultures influence people to mask or cover up ability weaknesses or deficiencies. There are many reasons for this influence:

- Fear of labels from management: being perceived as a person who "doesn't know how" is not desirable.

- Performance appraisals: most do not take into consideration learning curves, so people fear poor evaluations that can result from not knowing how to do something.

- Self assessments: society has not made it a positive attribute for adults to admit weaknesses and many fear the disapproval that might result.

For effective performance management, managers must recognize the reality of ability deficiencies that will occur due to entry level job placement, job change, promotions, organizational or workplace change initiatives, career moves, or organizational moves. Managers must make "not knowing how but willing to learn" a safe status for people to be in on a short-term basis and take appropriate leadership action in these situations that can turn potential and capability into real ability.

Leadership Action

When employees pass the litmus test for *ability deficiency* with respect to particular performance responsibilities—i.e., they, "couldn't do it if their life depended on it"—there are two basic situations the manager faces:

- Employee does not know how and knows it.
- Employee does not know how and doesn't know it.

The appropriate leadership action is to *TEACH* what needs to be taught.

Performance Question   Leadership Action

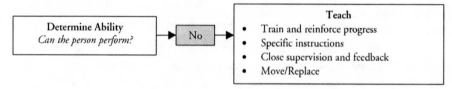

The following managerial behaviors represent the leadership action of *Teaching:*

- Provide formal training
- Hands on instruction: show and tell
- Specific guidance
- Close supervision

- Routine performance feedback
- Recognition and encouragement for progress
- Move to a more suitable job
- Replace

Teach to Remedy Ability Deficiencies

Avoid sink or swim situations where employees feel abandoned by the organization. This results in downward performance spirals and early resignation. Remember, employees leave managers, not organizations.

Training, teaching, and instruction are the only effective leadership behaviors that will have a positive impact on ability deficiencies. Everyone deserves the chance to "win" on the job, and managers who take the time to provide teaching for employees who need it can help develop win-win scenarios: wins for the organization, wins for the manager, and wins for employees.

Even when managers do not possess the specific or particular technical skills to teach employees how to do parts of their job, they have an obligation to give the employee access to those that can provide the training or relevant instruction.

The *Teach* leadership action provides employees with help and guidance that develops their potential. This action assists employees in overcoming any lack of confidence that might occur when faced with a new job or assignment. If they are assured that there is routine performance feedback relevant to acceptable standards, employees will have no doubts about their development progress when self-assessing their own performance. Taking the time to provide what is needed in the *Teach* process will eliminate many performance problems and save valuable time in the long run.

When employees with ability deficiencies do not respond well to appropriate training and coaching and performance stays consistently below desired standards, then managers should consider one of two options in the following order:

- Move the employee to another job that fits his or her suitability and potential.
- Replace the employee with someone else more eligible and suitable for the position.

Sacrificing the time, effort, and money of recruiting someone should not be considered if there is a spot in the organization that will enable the employee to perform and contribute. However, we recognize there are times when no other positions are available and when the eligibility and/or suitability of an employee isn't a performance fit for either the organization or the individual. In these cases, it is better for both parties in the long term to make a replacement move as soon as there is evidence of incompatibility.

Further, we recommend the process of probation hiring to all organizations. Probation hiring is creating a period of thirty to sixty or ninety days (no more than ninety) during which the employee is on performance probation. Depending on particular human resources practices, employees can be dismissed for suitability reasons, including evidence that they do not possess the potential capability for the job. During this period, it is imperative that the manager closely monitor all aspects of the employee's job so they can readily identify whether or not the employee can become successful in the position.

Probationary Hiring
• Term of thirty to ninety days
• Determine suitability and potential to perform
• Requires close supervision and attention
• The best attitude and behavior are seen during this period

If you have a probationary period for new hires, be careful of allowing employees who clearly do not posses the necessary potential for the position to work for the entire probationary period. Our interviews with many mangers have shown that the more time investment put into hoping an employee will become successful, the more apt the organization is to hang on to people who *can't* contribute in a meaningful manner. Further, allowing an employee to retain a position when he or she truly *can't* meet the required standards of the job does a disservice to the employee, other co-workers, and the organization.

Sometimes people can eventually learn the minimum required elements of a position. However, regarding attitude, you see a person's best behavior in the first thirty days. Much like a first date, you see the best attitude, the best

> ### The First Date
> *What you get during the first thirty days regarding attitude is normally the best you will see. Wishing and hoping for future improvement rarely pays off.*

behavior, the best manners, the best attire, and the best grooming in the first thirty days. If you're not pleased in the first thirty days, do not be so foolish as to hope for improvements in the future; it only goes downhill from there!

Termination during a probationary period for reasons of lack suitability or ability is really doing the employee a favor. If he or she is not really a fit for your organization, you will only be putting a square peg in a round hole. A more responsible action is to set the individual free to find a more suitable fit.

CHAPTER 5

Performance and Confidence

"Among other things, a leader must recognize the needs of the followers, help them see how these needs can be met, and give them the confidence that they can accomplish that result through their own efforts."

—Bernard Bass,
Leadership and Performance, Beyond Expectations

The third question using the *Performance Advantage Method* centers on the employee's attitude while performing the task or activity in question.

Performance Questions   Leadership Action

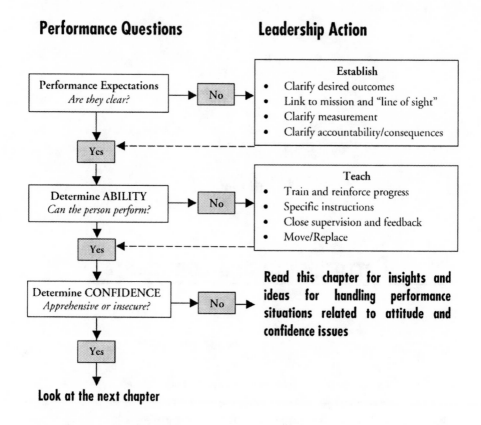

Look at the next chapter

Can Do, But Doesn't Do!

If employees have the ability to perform the desired job responsibility or assignment—they could perform routinely at the acceptable standard if their life depended upon it—and their work is unacceptable, then the leader is faced with an attitudinal problem. The employee, for some reason, won't perform satisfactorily. There are several performance situations that are unacceptable:

- **Performance Drifting South**
  The employee's performance is meeting the acceptable standard, but past performance was a standard higher than the present performance level.

  There are times when people who have performed at a superior level slip to performance levels below what they can do. While still maintaining performance at an acceptable standard, this employee is not giving his or her best effort.

- **Overdependent Performer**
  The employee's performance is acceptable, but the employee is still too dependent on the leader for support and encouragement.

  Sometimes employees develop the ability to perform at an acceptable level yet require substantial encouragement and support from the manager and seem hesitant to take personal responsibility for the job.

- **Marginal Performer**
  The employee's performance does not routinely meet the acceptable standard.

  This employee fluctuates between performance that meets the acceptable standard and performance that falls below standard. This up-and-down trend in performance usually signals the presence of some on-the-job or off-the-job problem situation that is affecting the employee.

- **Poor Performer**
  The employee's performance has dropped way below the acceptable standard.

  This situation is where performance has fallen off drastically. Performance that in the past was meeting acceptable standards is now consistently below standard.

When these situations occur and they are not caused by lack of ability, managers must take immediate action. Altering the employee's knowledge base, providing practice to gain experience, or skill development are not necessary alternatives. Remember, the employee has the necessary ability to perform. In these situations, managers must take action that will alter the conditions of the work environment, using consequence management if necessary, to uncover the reasons for the poor performance and select appropriate leadership intervention(s).

A Matter of Choice...

When attitude, not ability, is the reason for lack of acceptable performance, the central issue is a matter of *choice*. For some reason, the employee is *choosing* not to give his or her best efforts. Choice is what drives the human spirit. When people perform by choice, their efforts and talents produce significant results. When people perform because they feel compelled to, the results are usually disappointing. When people are *choosing* to withhold their best efforts, it is imperative to do one of the following:

(1). Alter the organizational conditions that are producing those choices, or if the employee chooses not to do his or her best because of personal issues,

(2). Terminate the employment relationship; otherwise, performance will continually remain at an unsatisfactory level and the attitudinal issue will become a cancer in the performance management process.

It is important to realize that in most instances employees choose to withhold their best efforts due to organizational issues, not because they have bad attitudes or don't care. As a matter of fact, often times the employees that care the most can be affected the most by organizational issues that cause insecurity, lack of commitment, and demotivation. In order to avoid neglecting the organizational issues that may be causing employees to choose to withhold best efforts, it is critical that managers uncover the reasons that these choices are being made. Merely labeling the situation as a performance problem and moving on to consequence management can amplify what is already an unsatisfactory situation and could rightly be termed *managerial malpractice*!

The question is "why is such a choice being made?" The answers are varied but can be found in six basic situations.

1. Confidence issues
2. Relevance issues
3. Performance barriers
4. Whose way is better
5. Consequence issues
6. Personal issues

Managerial Malpractice

In medicine, it is malpractice to prescribe and take action without accurate diagnosis of cause. In managing the performance of people, sadly enough, failure to identify cause accurately is often commonplace.

A further analysis of this list can be accomplished by identifying the attitudinal impact that results from these issues. There are three basic attitudinal outcomes for employees when they face these situations:

- Low Confidence
  - *Insecure* or *apprehensive* about their own performance
- Low Commitment
  - Failure to see the *importance, relevance,* or *impact* of their own performance
- Low Motivation
  - Lacks the *desire* to perform at an acceptable standard

Identifying the causal factor that is driving attitudinal responses in performance situations is the prerequisite action for solving or improving performance issues. One of the major problems in performance management is managerial action that is *not* related to the cause of the performance issue, that is, solutions that have no bearing on cause and effect (*remember the Beer Bust and Softball approach?*). When this happens, the unintended consequences of management action usually create a situation that is much worse than before action was taken. Over the years, we have noticed a common approach in handling performance issues.

Broken? Fix 'em!

When performance is unsatisfactory, the knee-jerk reaction is to look at the employee and determine how we can *fix* him or her. The employee is not performing well…he or she is *broken* and needs to be *fixed!* The result of that thinking is that something must be done *to* the employee to *repair* the situation. If the employee doesn't respond to the *fixing,* then the *damage* is deemed *beyond repair* and replacement of the "*totaled wreck*" is undertaken. This approach is fiscally irresponsible at best and extremely unfair to employees!

When employee performance slips or drops below the acceptable standard, the initial approach often is to determine what is *wrong* with the employee. The next step is to intervene with action that is directed at fixing what is wrong with the employee. Although sometimes dealing in this manner with employees is appropriate, most often the wrong lies elsewhere. Perhaps this happens so often because it is much simpler and more convenient to put the blame on employees for performance difficulties. The more difficult task, albeit the option that has a higher probability for success, is to take the time to uncover where the real problem does lie. The key is to identify the *reasons* that drive employee behavior, not merely respond to the resultant behavior.

There are numerous causes for performance issues other than employees. Here is a sampling:

- Unclear expectations
- Measuring the wrong things   ➜   *See Chapter Two*
- No understanding of importance of work

- Inadequate instruction or training
- Lack of feedback on progress   ➜   *See Chapter Three*

- Lack of recognition for accomplishment
- Dysfunctional policies or processes
- Inadequate resources
- Perceptions of inequity   ➜   *Read further*
- Punished for good work
- Lack of challenge
- Lack of responsibility

The above issues don't require the employee to be "fixed." Managerial behavior and work conditions are in question, and they must be addressed or altered. If not, then similar performance issues will recur with other employees and sustaining superior performance becomes a daunting task.

Confidence Issues

Employees can become apprehensive or insecure about their own ability for a number of reasons. When the lack of confidence results from lack of ability or inexperience, the appropriate leadership action is to *TEACH*. In such cases, it is the lack of ability that is driving the low confidence. No amount of encouragement, praising, rah-rah, or assurance can affect low confidence resulting from lack of ability. Without instruction, training, and guidance, the confidence will continue to falter. Lack of progress, failures in the learning process without corrective instruction, and lack of achievement will keep confidence at a low level. Remember that confidence and self-esteem are created through achievement, not "feel good" feedback! Revisit Chapter 3 for insights on dealing with ability issues that affect performance.

However, even when people have learned how to do a task or job function, confidence issues can arise. For some, fear of failure is a factor; for others, concern about responsibility or ownership of the job is a factor. For other individuals, it can be a set back or lack of progress, and some people can be unsure about their own ideas. It is very important for the manager to uncover confidence issues when they are affecting performance and to discover the cause of any insecurity or apprehension.

We remember talking with military pilots talking about flight school. They described themselves as extremely talented individuals who were handpicked for aviation. While possessing a deep desire and motivation to fly, they told of the knot in their gut when they were informed that they would solo for the first time. This apprehension or insecurity for taking on the sole responsibility for performance can be short-lived or it can continue to hinder development. The leadership action responding to confidence issues is a key factor in the performance management process.

Leadership Action

When it is apparent that an employee is

- *insecure* about his or her own performance; or
- *apprehensive* about taking personal initiative,

the appropriate leadership action is to **ENCOURAGE**. Being available for dialogue and discussion with the employee is necessary for these types of performance issues.

Performance Question   ## Leadership Action

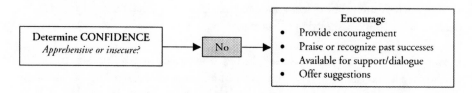

Here are some appropriate *Encourage* actions:

- When employees perform at an acceptable standard but
    - seem insecure about their own abilities,
        - provide performance feedback showing how well performance meets or exceeds standard
        - let employees know that you are pleased with their contribution
        - talk through the reasons an employees might have for their own perception
    - seem to be apprehensive or reluctant about taking personal initiative or responsibility,
        - provide feedback on your belief that they can handle the situation
        - reinforce their successful performance
        - praise and recognize any successful attempts regarding initiative
        - dialogue about employee concerns
    - are overly concerned about a mishap or mistake,
        - discuss and debrief the issue
        - reinforce their ability and past performance
        - use joint problem solving for the situation and agree on corrective action
    - lack the confidence in their own ideas or suggestions,
        - be available for dialogue
        - reinforce good ideas and suggestions

- encourage ideas and suggestions
- offer input and suggestions when necessary

A task of management is to develop people so they can perform *their* responsibilities on *their* own. Dealing with issues of insecurity and apprehension regarding autonomy, personal responsibility, and decision making (within the scope of a person's job) is a normal part of the managerial process. Taking the time to engage in the leadership actions that move employees from dependence on the manger to an independent or interdependent

> ### Avoid Dependence
>
> Unless lack of confidence is caused by lack of ability, providing instructions, how-to training, structure, and control will be counterproductive. Interventions of this type only create more *dependence* on the manager and do little to resolve the confidence issue. Superior performance results from a combination of ability and the willingness to own the job.

relationship regarding work responsibilities will result in higher levels of performance and job satisfaction, for both the employee and the manager.

CHAPTER 6

Performance and Commitment

"Because I said so!"
(the first sign of a dumb rule)

—George Carlin

The fourth question in the *Performance Advantage Method* regarding employee commitment is addressed in this chapter. There are times when employees just don't seem to understand the importance or relevance of the tasks they are asked to perform.

Performance Question   **Leadership Action**

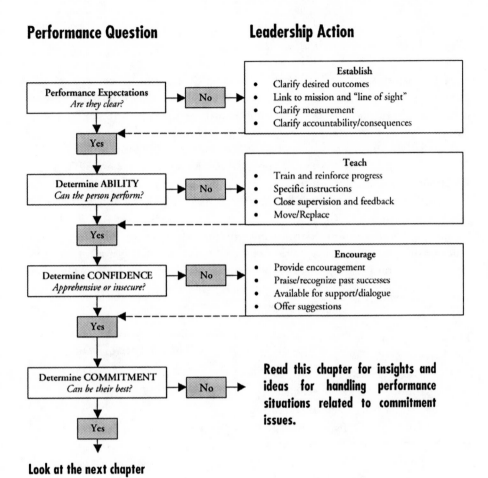

Look at the next chapter

Relevance Issues

The perception that the tasks people are asked to perform have no relevance leads to commitment issues for employees. This lack of commitment on the part of employees is many times due to organizational issues. In these situations, trying to improve employee performance without addressing these organizational issues produces less than desirable results. There are times when performance suffers because, although they know how to do what is asked of them, employees

- don't know *why* they must do things a particular way
- don't know the *importance* of the work they are asked to do

They don't know why they must do things a particular way:

Here we revisit an important lesson in creating clear performance expectations. Not only does this lack of knowledge about the reasons affect the clarity of what is expected, but it also affects the commitment that employees bring to their jobs. Ask employees, *"Why do you do it that way?"* How often do we hear, *"It's our policy."*? Follow up that answer with, *"Why is that the policy?"* You will often hear, *"I don't know I just work here,"* or some similar refrain as a response. These are situations where employees are performing duties with no knowledge of the relevance of the tasks and no understanding of why those duties are to be performed as they are. We again refer to the "line of sight" issue referred to in Chapter 2. You have to wonder just how long people can keep interested in any task or assignment when they didn't know why they are doing it a certain way. Also, inquiry must be made as to how embarrassed employees are when they must answer the inquiries with answers that explicitly illustrate that they don't know why they do things a certain way.

Most often in these circumstances, employees work for a manger who answers their questions about reasons with responses such as, "It's policy," or "Because I said so." The lingering assumption of this type of managerial response is that employees don't need a reason or understanding of why things are done a certain way because they are being paid to do what they are told, and the boss is the one charged with doing the telling.

> **The Absence of Why**
>
> *"Because I said so is the first sign of a dumb rule!"*
> George Carlin
>
> People can't be expected to demonstrate commitment when they don't know "why" they must do things the way they are asked.

Without the underlying reasoning and understanding, commitment and motivation suffer. People will trade time for money, but the effort and enthusiasm to do their best will not be present.

They don't know the importance of the work they are asked to do:

A major reason that tasks, duties, and responsibilities lack meaning and importance is because employees can't see a connection with what they are asked to do and the contribution it makes to the success of the organization. Without such a connection, work may well get done, but at what standard and with what level of interest or enthusiasm?

In The Looking Glass

How do you motivate people who perform boring, routine, mundane, "grunt" jobs? The answer is—you don't!

The problem is in the manager's assessment of (1) the nature of those jobs and (2) the type of people who must work those jobs.

Until the manager acknowledges the importance of all jobs that contribute to the success of an organization and acknowledges that any job done well done requires talent and effort, employee commitment toward those jobs will be lacking.

There are some jobs to which managers pay very little attention. This occurs when the job is basic, deemed as boring or routine, mundane, or requiring little skill. Often managers take the accomplishment of these jobs for granted. This neglect results in numerous performance pitfalls.

We were once asked by a restaurant manager for ideas on motivating people who performed boring, "grunt" jobs. There was nothing this manager could do to affect the performance and motivation of the people to whom he was referring. The problem here was not the employees; the problem was the manager and his assumptions about the task and the people. In asking how to "fix" the employees, he avoids the cause of his dilemma—his own mental model of that type of job and the type of people who would work that type of job. In certain situations, managers need to do some soul searching. If the job is worth paying for, it contains relevance and importance to the organization in some form. It is the responsibility of the manager to communicate that importance clearly and sincerely to those who are asked to perform the job.

Pat Riley, the National Basketball Association coach who led the Los Angeles Lakers to four world championships, once commented that his role was to ensure that the players knew and understood the importance of their contributions and received his appreciation for their efforts. His notion was that those players in the starring roles were taken care of by the fans and the media. He understood that every role, when done well, requires talent and effort. He wanted to make sure that the talent was recognized for what it was and that the effort was appreciated. He was spot on. We all know that in every job we can recall those who performed with excellence and those who were average and those who were below expectations. Managers must recognize the talent and effort necessary and make it clear that, for every job, talent and effort are noticed!

In all jobs, there is excellence to which certain employees aspire. Talent is not limited to sophisticated, high paying roles in the organization. Contribution is made on all levels. Many times, the roles that make the most impact on the customer are not the roles that are traditionally admired and respected in the organization. The effective manager realizes this and will make the effort to dignify and respect the outstanding effort of all in each and every role.

In other situations, employees are simply not clear on how what they do makes any difference to the organization's bottom line, business results, customer satisfaction, operational efficiency, and such. This is akin to playing sports without knowing how your efforts made a contribution to the objective of the game. Go ahead and bowl without pins, play golf in the dark, shoot basketball without a hoop, play football with no end zone. The effort would get old very fast!

> **How Long Would You Play?**
> - Bowl with no pins
> - Golf in the dark
> - Shoot basketball with no hoop
> - Play football with no end zone?
> - Play soccer with no goal?
>
> *Get the picture?*

> **Bowling with No Pins**
>
> *No connection between work efforts and contribution to the goals and objectives of the organization results in the employee activity of "trading time for money"!*

Perhaps that is why games, sports and certain hobbies are so attractive to so many; there is a clear understanding of how individual performance contributes to the outcome. Perhaps managers should attempt to make the conditions of work more reflective of the performance conditions of games, sports, and hobbies. It would surely provide a better understanding of the importance of the job! It would certainly give the employees a clear picture of whether or not their own performance makes a difference. And if the employees can't see whether any difference is made by the quality of their work, then what does it matter whether or not there is any difference in the quality of their efforts?

Commitment in any endeavor requires people to know how they make a difference. The accomplishment of job activities or tasks without any scorekeeping or feedback becomes boring at best and perhaps even frustrating and stressful.

Effective managers ensure that employees can answer the question, *"How do I contribute?" "How do I help the organization win?"* Under no conditions will they allow employees to perform tasks without making the appropriate connections between those tasks and the overall organizational objective. They do not dishonor their people by allowing them to feel as though their achievements serve no purpose. We've all been there and we all know how demoralizing and frustrating it can be to give our efforts and not get appropriate feedback on how those efforts make a contribution. Significance and meaning in work come from connecting the dots: I perform, I look at the results, and I want to know, "So what?"

Performance Barriers

Issues overlooked by those managing performance are performance obstacles that are not controlled by employees. The only effective intervention in these situations is to take quick and decisive action to remove the obstacle or barrier to good performance. Attempting to direct or motivate employees to improve performance when the cause is beyond their control is futile and eventually damages the manager-employee relationship. The employee senses that the manager as either out of touch or doesn't care. Either way, the problem not only persists, but eventually gets worse. Performance barriers can come from several sources:

- *Inadequate resources to do the job correctly:* lack of equipment, tools, or supplies from the standpoint of both quantity and quality, budget restrictions that restrict manpower, and outdated or ineffective software.

- *Policies that prevent employees from doing their best:* policies that were not designed to deliver the required output, policies that put employees into adversarial positions with customers, policies that bottleneck work accomplishment, and policies that don't foster internal cooperation between departments.

- *Work procedures that inhibit excellent performance:* inadequate information flow, managerial oversight that adds no value, intradepartmental goal and objective setting (with no regard for the effect on other departments), conflicting measurements or directives, measurements that conflict priorities, and ability to pass along defective work.

- *Information technology (IT) problems:* computer systems going down, system overloads, non-responsive IT support, and outdated hardware.

- *External occurrences:* weather difficulties, delivery failures, new competition, theft, power outages, etc.

When what is needed to support performance does not exist or when obstacles to performance occur, managerial action that attempts to "fix" the employee will be ineffective. When conditions that impair desired performance are out of the employee's control, the manager must take action that affects those conditions; nothing else will work.

We remember a sales conference at which a particular individual was awarded the top prize as salesman of the year. The numerous rewards, including the two-week trip to the Caribbean, were received with gratitude. However, when this top salesperson was asked by the vice president of sales to provide the rest of the group (those who didn't win) with

> **The External Factor**
>
> If the biggest storm that has hit Europe in the last five years destroys all the IT hardware of one of your very large customers. You too will have a great year and be on your way to the Caribbean for a couple of weeks.

some sterling comments of just how such excellence performance and resultant rewards were achieved, he readily declined (you might wonder why he would share his performance secrets with those to whom he might lose next year). When forced on stage to provide words of wisdom, he made the following speech (paraphrased):

"Well, ok, how did I do it? Perhaps you might want to write down my five step sales process. First, I was fortunate to have what we term a 'mega territory,' which means that 75% of you won't have the chance to win. Second, in my mega territory I had what we term a 'mega customer,' which means that several of the remaining 25% of you won't win either. Third, I was fortunate enough to have the largest storm that hit Europe land in the vicinity of my mega customer. Fourth, there just happened to be a leak in the roof of my mega customer's business which flooded the IT area. Fifth, this customer had mostly competitive products at the time, fortunately for me, because we don't get credit nearly as much for repeat business as we do for new business. Oh, yes, one other item, the sales rep from my major competition was a real jerk! If you have all those variables in place next year, you will be standing in my place. Thank you."

Needless to say, the vice president was not very pleased with this presentation. This is not a story to discredit excellent performance; the sales person was very good at what he did. However, to contrast the performance of others against his performance and to challenge others to rise to his level by harder work, more dedication, or individual effort when external factors played such a big role was ludicrous and would have made management seem way out of touch. Many times, factors beyond the employee's control inhibit desired performance; other times, such as that just described, foster desired performance. Either way, managers need to become adept at understanding the real cause and effect on performance issues if they are to become effective in influencing performance in a positive manner.

Present day managers faced these issues routinely when they were still in the position of being employees. Why is it that we forget these influences on performance when we become managers and look directly to the employees as the causes? Why is it that many of the *causes* of performance are not understood by managers? Perhaps, as employees, we face the *immediate consequences* of inappropriate policies, inadequate resources, inhibiting work procedures, and such. This issue is important. We learn best from the consequences of our actions. When our actions are quickly followed by negative consequences, we have both of the following:

- Urgency to change how things are done
- The desire to change how things are done

However, when our actions are not shortly followed by negative consequences, when individuals other than ourselves are immediately affected, or when the direct consequences of our actions are never readily apparent, then we lack both the urgency and desire to change, and most often we don't even understand what is working well to support desired performance and what isn't.

The following example will serve to illustrate how learning is fostered or inhibited by the timeliness of consequences. When you touch a hot stove with a finger, the finger is quickly removed because the sensation of pain is quickly communicated to the brain through the nerves. The consequence of pain is immediate and the corrective action is taken immediately. Perhaps you might attempt to touch the hot stove a second time to determine whether the incident was a random occurrence, whether the pain was in fact caused by the action taken. A couple of attempts at touching the stove are really all that are necessary before the behavior is altered permanently.

Consider the following. Suppose that you touch a hot stove, and your finger is burning, but you can't feel the sensation of pain and you can't see the burning effect. What if it would take nine to ten months for the sensation to travel the nerve pathways to your brain before any painful sensation would register? What if it took nine to ten months for the skin to begin to redden from repeated touches to the stove? The action that causes the problem would most likely continue. Not only that, if the pain did finally appear but you were not touching the stove at the time the pain did register, then you would most likely look at your present activity or situation to determine the cause. This is considered a learning disability. And this type of learning disability is very prevalent in organizations.

The Manager's Learning Disability

When managers don't suffer the consequences of their actions and decisions in real time, they lack

- the understanding of performance influencers,

- the urgency to change, and

- the desire to change.

Result? They tend to defend their decisions and actions and find fault with others for poor performance.

Many managers suffer from this learning disability. The decisions about policies, work procedures, resources, IT support, etc. are normally made by managers. The people who are directly affected, day in and day out, by those decisions are the employees. Consider the employee who must perform under an unfriendly customer policy. Who continually takes the "heat" from the unhappy customer? Who is put in the position of constantly defending an inconvenient way of doing business? Whose motivation at work suffers? Who gets the label of "complainer" when trying to bring the policy problem to management attention?

Managers, day in and day out, are not the ones who have to deal with the consequences of many of their decisions or policies and thus they

- are not sensitized to the cause and effect of performance issues.

- do not learn what is helpful and what is not.

Touch the Stove

Managers need to experience the consequences of their actions and decisions that affect employee performance and customer experience in order to gain an understanding of what things support performance and what things don't!

- tend to continue to defend their decisions (if only employees would just give a better effort).

After spending lengthy customer moments of insanity in voice mail jail or with employees who are encumbered by surrealistic policies or procedures, we often wonder why members of the executive team don't take the time to call their own 800 numbers or experience their own organization in exactly the same manner as we do. We know that if they did, work processes and practices would be changed in a heartbeat. However, we have given in to the fact that, in most cases, the managers who create the policies and practices never have to experience them. When they deal with their own organization, they receive special treatment.

Several years ago when Bob Small took over as vice president of Resort Hotels at Disney World, he put a system in place in which his hotel managers, when creating a new policy or work procedure, would have to work under and personally experience the consequences of their decisions. He did this to ensure that the desired results of new policies were actually achieved and to determine what, if any, unintended consequences were created. We find this to be a very sound practice which will lead to the prevention of many performance problems before they occur.

There is one more procedural issue that we can't overlook. This is the barrier to performance that results from managerial action regarding the oversight or sign-off procedures they use in approving certain aspects of employee work activity. We favor any approval procedure when value is created for the customer or organization as a result of the approval. However, when no value is added in any way from an approval procedure, when it is done for the sake of control with no definable advantages, the effect on employee motivation is negative and performance can suffer.

Take the example we've all experienced, cashing a check. The employee makes you wait for a manager's approval. When the manager arrives, he or she signs the check *without looking* at it! Your time was wasted if all that was required was a signature without any idea of what that signature was approving—*anyone* could have signed the approval. More importantly, the effect on the employee is counterproductive as well because the employee is most likely *embarrassed* by having the customer notice that he or she isn't allowed to do something a manager or supervisor can do without so much as looking, much less do *without any type of thought process* at all..

Additionally, this managerial behavior is very *demeaning* to the employee. The action communicates the lack of trust the organization has in the employee by not allowing the employee to do something it allows the manager or supervisor to do without any criteria or thought. We have often empathized with what is going through the employee's mind: "I could have done that myself!", "If having no thought process is the criterion for management, I qualify!" What can we expect from employees when managerial actions signal low respect and trust? What can we predict about employee attitude when managerial actions insult and demean? We are constantly amazed at how many times we see this type of managerial behavior and even more amazed that managers are unaware of the effect.

When this type of work occurrence is routine, employees eventually lose their motivation to perform well. They simply go through the motions and, if they can't afford to leave the job, they begin trading time for money. When their nonchalant attitude is visible to management, it is the employees that are deemed in need of "fixing." How far will manager exhortations regarding high performance go? How about an employee of the month program to improve morale? When all else fails, a beer bust and softball game is always a possibility! Let's be really clear: the *only action* that will improve employee performance in these situations is a change in managerial procedures.

Leadership Action

When employees don't see the *relevance* or *importance* of what they are being asked to do and when they are *blocked* from doing their best, the appropriate leadership action is to *INSPIRE*. Provide clarification and understanding of the importance and relevance of required tasks and ways of doing things. Create the "line of sight" for employees by illustrating how their performance affects other people. Remove barriers and obstacles that prevent employees from doing their best. Take the time to experience the job in exactly the same manner as the employee does, thereby learning the unintended consequences of performance. Eliminating performance obstacles and reinforcing the importance and dignity of a person's job *inspires* outstanding performance.

Performance Question   Leadership Action

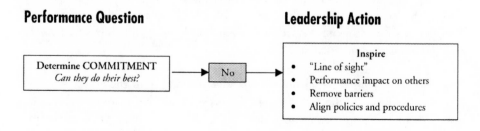

Here are some appropriate *INSPIRE* actions for dealing with *relevance* issues. When employees have the ability to perform at an acceptable standard yet do not put forth the effort necessary to perform with excellence:

- ✓ Discuss and clarify the gap between the desired performance level and the present level.
- ✓ Engage in open-ended questions* to discover the reasons for the lack of effort.
- ✓ Take a nonjudgmental* stance in initially discussing the performance issues and reasons for the present state.
- ✓ Use "I" messages* to convey your feelings and understanding of the situation
- ✓ Reinforce the importance of tasks and assignments.
- ✓ Create the "line of sight" so that employees clearly understand how their performance affects other people.
- ✓ Create a process for providing routine performance feedback on how well the task or assignments are being performed and the impact of the performance.

Here are some appropriate *INSPIRE* actions when dealing with *performance barriers*. When employees have the ability to perform at an acceptable standard yet do not put forth the effort necessary to perform with excellence:

- ✓ Discuss and clarify the gap between the desired performance level and the present level.
- ✓ Be open to the issues that employees face when performing in a specified manner; use open-ended questions.
- ✓ Take the time to work a shift (or short time) under the conditions that employees report are causing difficulties.
- ✓ Get customer feedback on how the "way" you do business affects the customer's experience.
- ✓ Get an understanding for the consequences to the organization and the employee resulting from identified performance barriers.

* Our book and training program, "*The Coaching Advantage*," provides ideas, insights, and skills that create performance competencies and improve face-to-face performance discussions.

✓ Create a routine information flow to all feedback regarding the effect of policies, procedures, resources, management practices, etc.

✓ Provide appreciation to those who bring performance barrier issues to your attention.

When managers are naïve or oblivious to the barriers that inhibit superior performance, employees tend to see management as not really caring about their work situation. Fighting the windmills in a Don Quixote method of goal accomplishment gets old fast. Performance suffers and really talented people look for other opportunities. Recognizing that commitment problems normally result from managerial or organizational issues—and not from the character of the employees—is an important part of the performance management process.

Managerial *enthusiasm* over the quality of every job and the *structures of measurement and feedback* regarding the performance of jobs *invites* the commitment of employees. With this invitation, the employee makes the commitment choice. Many times, the performance issue is resolved with such leadership action. When employees fail to choose commitment in spite of clarity about the importance of what they are asked to do, then the manager must deal with the personal motivation factors that affect performance.

CHAPTER 7

Performance and Desire

"The only place success comes before work is in the dictionary!"

—Vince Lombardi

The fifth question in the *Performance Advantage Method* concerns employee desire and motivation. What if employees lack the desire to perform well? What if they just don't *want* to do a good job?

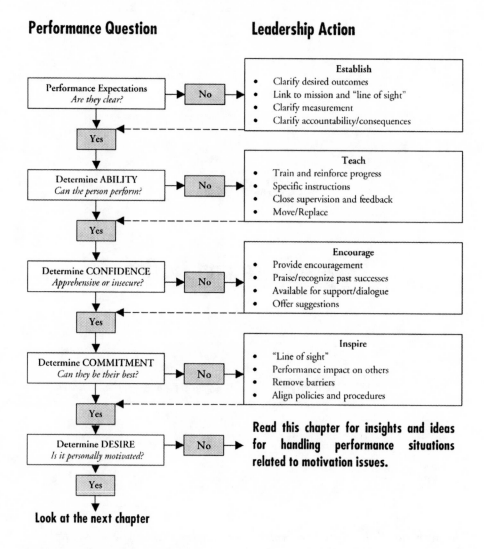

Performance Question

Performance Expectations
Are they clear?

No → **Establish**
- Clarify desired outcomes
- Link to mission and "line of sight"
- Clarify measurement
- Clarify accountability/consequences

Yes

Determine ABILITY
Can the person perform?

No → **Teach**
- Train and reinforce progress
- Specific instructions
- Close supervision and feedback
- Move/Replace

Yes

Determine CONFIDENCE
Apprehensive or insecure?

No → **Encourage**
- Provide encouragement
- Praise/recognize past successes
- Available for support/dialogue
- Offer suggestions

Yes

Determine COMMITMENT
Can they be their best?

No → **Inspire**
- "Line of sight"
- Performance impact on others
- Remove barriers
- Align policies and procedures

Yes

Determine DESIRE
Is it personally motivated?

No → **Read this chapter for insights and ideas for handling performance situations related to motivation issues.**

Yes

Look at the next chapter

Leadership Action

Whose Way Is Better?

We know that when employees don't believe in or trust the way things are done, their best efforts are not applied to the job. Yet, we've all been in situations where the way we were asked to do things ranged at best from silly to clearly stupid. We've all scratched our heads at times and wondered why on earth we were doing something a certain way. Our feelings in those situations cover the gambit of emotions:

- ✓ This is idiotic.
- ✓ Who is the moron who made this decision?
- ✓ This is hopeless.
- ✓ If they want it done this way, they must not care about (fill in the blank).

The quality of performance and the level of effort are always inhibited as a result of these emotions. Why would people do their best when they don't believe their best is achievable under prevailing situations? This question must be addressed by managers. Constructive dialogue and explanations regarding the way things are done are critical for influencing outstanding performance. Ignoring employee concerns about the

> **And I did it...*MY WAY.***
> - My way is better.
> - Your way won't work.
> - Your way doesn't work.
> - My way is just as good as yours.
>
> The dilemma of how to do tasks!

best way to do things and trumping their questions with authoritative managerial decrees put both performance and employee motivation at risk.

Insight and ideas about better ways of doing things come from various employee sources:

- ✓ Employees who have been around and understand why certain things don't work.
- ✓ Experienced employees who gain an understanding about what changes can provide better results.
- ✓ New employees with a fresh perspective who don't understand why things are done the way they are.

First, clearly there are times when employees who routinely perform tasks experience difficulties. Having to deal with these difficulties sensitizes people to look for corrective actions. As a result, better ways of doing things are developed that would be impossible in an atmosphere of closed door management decisions. When employees are encouraged to look for better ways of doing things and they are listened to, two beneficial by-products occur:

1. Improvements in practices are developed and implemented.

2. Meaningful participation in the work process by the employee is achieved.

This second point cannot be overemphasized. To reiterate, one of the reasons talented people choose to do their best and to stay with an organization is the level of *meaningful participation* they are afforded in tasks and policies that affect their daily work life!

Second, sometimes a fresh pair of eyes that are not burdened by tradition or the experience of "the way we've always done it" can be beneficial. New employees have not been conditioned or socialized to the company status quo. They don't know the rhetorical answers to the question "Why do we do it this way?" They bring interesting questions to bear on present practices. Managers have a choice: use this source of inquiry advantageously or write off the comments because the source is new. The manager's choice in this matter will set the *tone* for all new employees who make an assumption that their voice regarding improvement does or doesn't matter!

> ### Deflators
>
> *Managerial pronouncements that lack explanation and relevant facts disenfranchise the mind and kill the human spirit.*

Employees who have better ways of doing things are a blessing: the attitude to seek improvement is not something that should be in any way *deflated*. When managers are open to new ideas, not only do better ways of performing tasks get implemented, but employees become motivated to look continually for ways to continually improve. Yet there are many *deflation* tactics that managers adopt automatically when their way is challenged or questioned.

- "When you've been here awhile, you'll understand."
- "That's the way we've always done it."
- "Look, trust me; this is the best way."
- "Because I said so."

These statements simply won't work. For the life of us, we cannot understand why many managers continue to rely on these types of pronouncements in response to employee inquiry. They certainly *won't inspire* people to give their best. They don't *answer* the question about the best way to do things. When these answers are forced upon people, it is an arbitrary exercise of position power and nothing more. "I'm the boss…just do it" is the message. Is this really the desired outcome of employee inquiry and attempts to improve work practices?

This is not to say that all critiques of present ways of doing things are helpful. Many times, present practices are the best way. In any case, the manager has the obligation to contrast present practices with recommended ones, to identify the advantages of either, to identify the unintended consequences of recommended practices, and to explain in full why the present practice is the beneficial choice. Why wouldn't any manager want to have this discussion with employees about how the work is to be carried out? As important as employee talent is, *employee confidence* in the ways and methods of doing their work is just as important.

The following is a managerial check list for dealing with "best way" issues:

- Is the present way the best?
    - Do you have the *criteria* that prove it?
- Is the recommended way better?
    - What are the *criteria* to prove it?
- Will the recommended way fail to work?
    - What are the *criteria* to prove it?
    - What are the *unintended consequences* that prohibit trial?
- Is the recommended way equal in outcome to the present practice?
    - Is it really *important* that the employee do it a specific way?

Sometimes new ways of doing things seem to be better yet, with closer examination, negative implications become apparent. What will save time and money might very well have negative consequences with customers. Productivity gains may well be accompanied by excessive costs. Efficiency gains could come at the expense of customer satisfaction, negative impacts on other employees, or other departments. Sometimes safety issues can be put at risk with new ways

> **Criteria for looking at new ways of doing things:**
> ✓ Impact on customers
> ✓ Productivity gains
> ✓ Efficiency gains
> ✓ Impact on other employees or departments
> ✓ Safety issues
> ✓ Costs

that provide attractive results. Managers must look at the interactive relationship of all-important criteria when considering new ways of doing things. The result of the analysis should be shared with employees so everyone understands why things are done the way they are.

With pertinent information and considerate explanation, we move beyond personal opinion and coercion regarding how to do things and reach consensus about the best practices. Employee desire is affected to the extent that managers apply thoughtful consideration to doing things better. This is healthy for the organization and the employee and increases the level of employee performance.

Leadership Action

When differences over the *way* things should be done occur, the appropriate leadership action is to *INQUIRE* o determine the issues, and then to *SUPPORT* by consideration of present practices and explanation of reasoning for the present procedures.

Performance Questions   **Leadership Action**

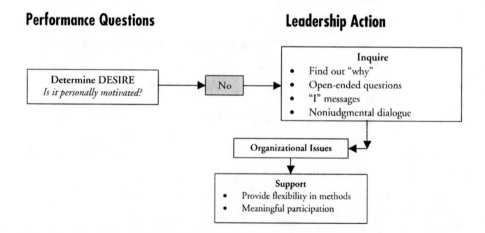

Here are some appropriate *INQUIRE* and *SUPPORT* actions when dealing with differences in *how* things should be done:

* When employees have the ability to perform at an acceptable standard yet do not put forth the effort necessary to perform with excellence:

✓ Discuss and clarify the gap between the desired performance level and the present level.

✓ Engage in open-ended questions to discover the reasons for the lack of effort.

✓ Take a nonjudgmental stance in initially discussing the performance issues and reasons for the present state.

✓ Use "I" messages to convey your feelings and understanding of the situation.

✓ Gain an understanding of the employee's dissatisfaction with the present way of doing things

✓ Provide explanation of the relevant business reasons for present ways of doing things.

✓ Consider new ways of performing the work in question.

✓ Provide appreciation to those who show initiative regarding improving the way things are done.

Managing Consequences

"How many times do I have to tell you?"

"If I have to tell you one more time, there's going to be trouble."

Perhaps I wasn't clear last time…I want this to be the last time I have to tell you."

If this series of interventions was thought to be something that would elicit any change in behavior, the provider was sadly mistaken. Even if we consider that, at each intervention, the emotions increased or the voice volume increased, in reality it's just noisy clutter to the recipient. It is incredible how many times people fall prey to behavior that is the result of their own mismanagement of consequences. As managers and even as parents, we have all been prey!

We travel now to the days of yesteryear when the plethora of scientific evidence began to mount and continues to this day supporting the idea that behavior is a function of *consequences*! What do we know?

• Behavior frequency is increased when the behavior is followed by a positive consequence.

- Behavior frequency is diminished when the behavior is followed by a negative consequence.

What's in It For the Employee?
• No positive consequence for doing it right.
• No negative consequence for doing it wrong.
• Positive consequence for not doing it right.
• Negative consequence for doing it right.
Falling prey to one's own mismanagement of consequences is a typical managerial dilemma.

So, armed with this knowledge, managers can overcome many employee motivational and desire difficulties by applying this insight to performance situations. What are the positive consequences that result from superior performance? What are the negative consequences that result from less than desirable performance? Are there any positive consequences for performing at a poor level? Are there any negative consequences for performing at a superior level? For many managers, the answers to these questions can be surprising. To understand truly the issues involved, these performance consequence situations must be considered from the employees' point of view.

What are the positive consequences that result from superior performance?

When jobs or tasks have some inherent benefit to the employee—learning, challenge, personal enjoyment, etc.—intrinsic motivation is working for both the employee and the manager. However, many tasks don't contain this inherent benefit. As a manager, you become the source of positive consequences. The possibilities are many, but you must ensure that superior performance provides positive consequences to the employee. Here are some suggestions:

- Performance feedback indicating how performance impacts organizational goals and objectives: this communicates the level of *contribution* of the employee.

- Routine performance feedback that indicates how well the employee is performing relative to standard: this indicates the level of personal *achievement* of the employee.

- Supporting the employee with warranted high performance marks on performance appraisals or performance evaluations: this indicates organizational *acknowledgment* for high performance and makes the employee *competitive* for future assignments.

- Support for the employee for warranted promotions: this indicates the manager's *commitment* to the employee in reward for the employee efforts.

- Investment in the best tools or resources for the employee to perform with: this indicates managerial *support* for the employee's best efforts.

- Assign desirable assignments and projects to those who are deserving: this indicates a *reward* for sustainable excellence.

- Routine personal recognition and praise from the manager referencing the employees' efforts: this indicates *appreciation* and *awareness* of the extra efforts.

- Support for merit increases, bonuses when appropriate, and pay increases when possible: this indicates *acknowledgment* of employee value.

- Ensure that recognition and rewards for performance are not in relation to what each employee does but relative to a standard of high expectations or standards: this indicates that *superior performance is valued*, not employee competition.

These are just some of the many ideas we have gleaned from interviews and assessments with managers and employees over the years. You can probably add several of your own from your past experiences.

What are the negative consequences that result from less than desirable performance?

When the reasons for poor performance—such as lack of ability, performance barriers, lack of importance or relevance, lack of confidence, or low confidence in practices—have been identified and dealt with appropriately, it is time to look at the consequence issue. When employees perform at a level below the standard, there must be some accompanying level of discomfort. Without *accountability* for poor performance, a superior performance culture in a company is unattainable. Remember, one of the more demotivating factors in a work environment is having to work side by side with a non-performer. Worse yet is a situation in which the manager is aware and yet does nothing about it! Also remember, if the speed limit is 65 mph but the tolerance is 75 mph, everybody will be going 75 mph because *tolerance* for any given level of performance is a positive consequence for that behavior.

Some examples of negative consequences for poor performance* are the following:

- Immediate intervention when poor performance is noticed: this indicates that management is *on top of things* and will not give any leeway.

- Clear expectations for improvement, agreed upon by the employee, in order to avoid future discipline: this indicates that punishment is not the first alternative, but that *corrective action* is the focus.

- An assignment in which the employee must research the effects and implications of his or her poor performance and provide a learning report on why such performance is problematic and what corrective action should be taken: this indicates a desire to provide clarity to the employee on the *consequences of poor performance* to the organization and to other employees.

- Personal reprimands for poor performance citing the performance issue, the implications, and required corrective action: this indicates an expectation of *firmness* in dealing with poor performance.

- Refusal to provide desirable work assignments when performance is poor this indicates *integrity* in the accountability process.

- Refusal to support inappropriate recommendations for transfer assignments or promotions: this indicates that poor performers will *not be given a free pass* to other departments at the expense of good performers who are more deserving.

- Eliminate multiple chance opportunities: this indicates that poor performance will not be *tolerated*.

- Follow through on the required progressive discipline or personnel disciplinary processes of the company or organization: this indicates a *commitment to superior performance* and support of those that do perform well.

- Remove those performers who continue to perform poorly and contaminate the work environment: this indicates the *serious nature* of performance and organizational success.

* These are recommendations gleaned from interviews and assessments with employees and managers; not all of them fall under the allowances in the framework of some personnel regulations. Check with your human resources department for assistance on what is available to you.

Remember, the meaning of discipline comes from the term "disciple" defined as a learner. The route of negative consequences should follow the path of constructive discipline: teaching the employee the error of this or her ways and providing an avenue for corrective action. Although punishment or firing is sometimes in order, it is not the first step in the process of redirecting performance.

Here is an important item to remember. Don't confuse negative consequences with the example leading off this section. Continual begging and pleading, even when done with anger and a loud voice, becomes nothing more than a routine irritant to those on the

> *Freeway Noise*
>
> *This is management noise that ultimately contains no consequence, positive or negative, and gets tuned out due to the continual, mind-numbing reoccurrence combined with lack of follow through!*

receiving end; it does nothing to alter performance behavior. It becomes *freeway noise!* We have friends that live next to a freeway. When we visit, we ask how they deal with the noise coming from the freeway. They reply, "What noise?" It is so routine and commonplace they no longer hear it. This rule applies to lack of managerial follow through!

Are there any positive consequences for performing at a poor level?

As funny as it may seem, there are sometimes positive consequences for performing at poor levels. We've all heard stories of "rate-buster" experiences. At times, superior performers can receive harassment from those who are not willing to do their best. When superior performance is not followed by positive consequences, employees can fall *victim* to unwanted positive consequences from other sources.

Managers can even reward poor performance with positive consequences accidentally. I was once in a situation in which the poor performance of special projects and collateral assignments was met with the poor performer not being given any more of these collateral duties. The fact was that these collateral duties took time away from primary job responsibilities which were given paramount consideration for performance review and promotion opportunities. It was little wonder that this practice of eliminating those who performed poorly on collateral assignments from similar future assignments was perceived as a *positive consequence* in the eyes of the poor performer.

> ### Transfer the Problem
>
> *The management tactic of avoiding confrontation of performance problems by transferring or promoting the poor performer sends a message: "Screw up and get what you want!"*

Another situation in which managers fall victim to poor consequence management is when transfers or promotions go only to those who can be "spared." This creates the feeling among employees that doing your best is punished and doing less than your best is rewarded. Keeping the best talent static and providing movement to the lesser talented people are formulas for destroying a performance culture. Yet, we see examples of this often!

The following are some examples of positive consequences for poor performance that should be eliminated:

- Non-assignment of extra tasks or responsibilities for poor performers (while giving these to only the best performers): this indicates that poor performance allows employees to *avoid* extra work and that the worse they perform, the less they will have to do. (Note: the taking on of additional tasks and responsibilities when *necessary* should be an element of *everyone's* job.)

- Paid days off when employees are suspended for poor performance: this indicates that poor performance results in *being paid* for doing nothing.

- No consequences for being late because the employee slept late: this indicates that the consequence for being late is *more sleep*.

- In absence of positive attention for good performance, the employee receives managerial attention for poor performance: this indicates that poor performance is the way to get some *recognition*, even if it is negative. Remember, any recognition or attention is better than none.

- Transfers or promotions going to employees who are not the best performers: this indicates that the way to get ahead or get out of a particular work situation is to *fail to do your best*.

- Receiving benefits (time off, doughnut mornings, pizza Fridays, company parties) as morale and performance boosters prior to performance improvement: this indicates that poor performance results in *positive activities* without having to earn them.

- Allowing continued excuses for poor performance with no requirement for eliminating the poor performance: this indicates that excuses are *rewarded* with a lack of accountability.

Whenever it is comfortable to perform poorly, when employee status is maintained even in light of poor performance, or when something beneficial happens as a result of performing poorly, the consequences are working in favor of continued poor performance. This lesson is simple: *behavior that results in a positive consequence will be repeated.* When this behavior is poor performance, the poor performance *will* continue! The employee's performance will not change unless the consequences are changed.

Are there any negative consequences for performing at a superior level?

There are times when the extra effort needed for superior performance isn't worth the giving. As alluded to previously, not only does the removal of assignments from poor performers reward those performers, the additional work that then gets assigned to good performers can serve as a negative consequence. Overburdened with more work as a result of doing a good job, while others get off easy due to their lack of effort, top performers began to feel taken advantage of and learn to decrease their efforts or look for other organizations that will respond fairly to their efforts. "Quit and stay or quit and leave" is the mantra for those whose exceptional performance is taken lightly or, worse, treated unfairly.

Avoid the trap of making outstanding effort not worth the effort. As a new employee, I once worked with a fellow who worked so poorly that that the term "subpar" was equated with excellence! Being a new employee, I was determined to show my mettle to my supervisor. I worked hard, doing my part while my co-worker worked at his usual pace, (I would use the term "snail's pace," but that would be insulting to snails.) My supervisor was so pleased with my work that he continued to tell me to help my co-worker with his work. I was new, so I was a bit slow on the uptake, but I did learn. My new employee enthusiasm and motivated efforts quickly altered and my supervisor unwittingly created a *clone* of my co-worker.

> **Less for Worse?**
> **More for Better?**
>
> • The worse you do, the less you are asked to do.
>
> • The better you do, the more you are asked to do.
>
> The result? Good performers are asked to carry the load for poor performers while both get paid the same! This is not a good deal!!!

Some examples of how superior performance can receive negative consequences are the following:

> ### Can't Afford to Lose You
> *Management tactic of refusing to promote or transfer their best people, thus sending the message that superior performance and extra effort will get you nowhere.*

- When the reward for superior performance is more work, while poor performers get a pass, this indicates that extra effort just results in *more work*.

- When good performance is met with co-worker criticism or harassment, this indicates that the prevailing performance culture is to *withhold* performance.

- When transfers and promotions are withheld from excellent performers under the guise "We can't afford to lose you," the hard worker gets the message that the *extra effort* won't bring promotion or positive change.

- When performance evaluation marks must be randomly distributed among employees rather than given for a standard of performance, this indicates that excellence in performance might not receive its just reward and that rewards don't follow from effort: the marks might be *punishing* rather than rewarding.

Superior performance must be worthwhile to the employee for it to be sustained. Your role as a manager is to manage consequences accordingly. Get a handle on this and increase your success and fulfillment as a manager.

Leadership Action

When consequences for performance are in question, the appropriate leadership action is to **INQUIRE** about the consequences or lack thereof in the specific situation, to **SUPPORT** by creating positive consequences and removing negative consequences for superior performance, and **ENFORCE** by holding poor performers accountable and eliminating positive consequences for poor performance.

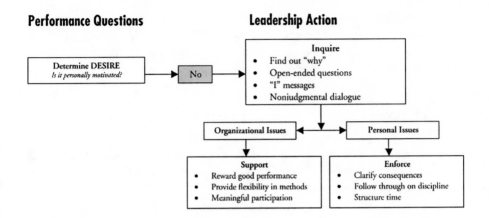

Here are some appropriate *INQUIRE, SUPPORT,* and *ENFORCE* actions for dealing with *performance consequences*:

- When employees have the ability to perform at an acceptable standard yet do not put forth the effort necessary to perform with excellence:
    - ✓ Get clarity about the performance gap, the present state vs. the desired state.
    - ✓ Engage in open-ended questions to discover the reasons for the lack of effort.
    - ✓ Take a nonjudgmental stance in initially discussing the performance issues and reasons for the present state.
    - ✓ Use "I" messages to convey your feelings and understanding of the situation.
    - ✓ Get an understanding for the consequences that occur under the performance issue in question.
    - ✓ Take action to eliminate positive consequences for poor performance and negative consequences for superior performance.
    - ✓ Commit to holding poor performers accountable.
    - ✓ Intervene and hold people accountable for putting pressure on good performers to reduce their performance levels.
    - ✓ Ensure that superior performance is never ignored.
    - ✓ Commit to creating positive consequences for superior performance.

Many performance problems can be overcome when the manager diligently adheres to the science of behavior. People will *continue* to do the things for which they receive positive consequences and they will *stop* doing the things for which they receive negative consequences. This is a simple but true principle!

Personal Issues

There are times when employees lose their motivation to do their job well because of personal reasons. There are two common situations involving a drop in motivation to perform well:

- When personal problems arise in the employee's life
- When the job becomes boring or loses its enjoyment

When personal problems occur in the employee's life

Outside problems can affect the employees' ability to focus or concern themselves with their performance efforts. These are difficult situations for managers to deal with. If handled inappropriately, problems for the employee, manager, and organization can be increased as a result. For the majority of these problems, managers aren't equipped or skilled enough to be able to deal with them effectively. Many times, when managers try, things only get worse.

Managers need to be sensitive, empathetic, and firm simultaneously when confronting performance issues that result from personal problems. No one is immune to an outside problem, which can strike anyone, at any time. Rare is the individual whose performance doesn't suffer to some extent as a result of dealing with outside problems. The way managers must deal with these issues is dependent on the degree to which the outside problem is affecting the employee's job performance. Many times, human resources departments can provide assistance to managers on how to deal with performance problems resulting from outside problems. Employee assistance programs are, in many cases, a beneficial alternative source for the employee. Managers should become informed about the help that is available to employees when their performance suffers due to outside problems.

The Outside Problem

- Divorce
- Alcohol
- Drugs
- Family medical issues
- Child care issues
- Transportation issues
- Financial problems

These are some of the problems that tend to have lasting negative effects on performance. Once these factors appear as causal influencers on performance, intervention is usually necessary.

Outside problems that affect employee performance can range from issues as significant as divorce to those as seemingly trivial as a disagreement with a neighbor. When people have to deal with the effects of divorce or alcohol, drug or substance abuse, death of a loved one, financial difficulties, lack of adequate child care, and the like, they can lose their focus and their immediate personal problems become the important influencers of behavior. This becomes a dilemma as the employee struggles with the outside problem. This struggle can have such a negative impact on job performance that their job can be in jeopardy. This job jeopardy can make it even more difficult for the employee to deal effectively with the outside problem. You can readily see the problems inherent in this situation.

Clearly, once the effects of the outside problem begin to affect an employee's job performance, the ability of the person to turn things around without some type of intervention is extremely rare. Getting the necessary assistance to deal effectively with the outside problem is many times a prerequisite to saving the person's job as well.

Sometimes assistance can be provided with time off work, flexible hours, or some other alternative to accommodate the situation. However, the obligation and responsibility for acceptable performance which the employees has to the organization *does not disappear* as a result of the outside problem. Accommodation sometimes facilitates the commitment of the employee to ensure that performance will return to a reasonable level. Other times, however, directing the employee to seek professional assistance (with the help of the human resources department) is the only way to save the person's job.

Don't fall into the trap of trying to be a personal counselor to employees by offering advice on how they should handle things in their personal life. This is the road of good intentions that leads to…well, let's just say you don't want to venture in this direction. You are most likely not qualified or credentialed in the arena in which the employee is having difficulties. Your expertise is *performance* and you must stay in that arena. Although you can be accommodating to the degree that your organizational policies allow, you must be very clear on the requirements for the job to be performed correctly. If this necessitates professional help, remember that you are not the professional in this matter. Direct the employee to seek assistance, if that what it is going to take to get performance back on track.

When the job becomes boring and/or loses its enjoyment

Sometimes people simply lose interest in their job. The routine of the job becomes boring, the challenge in the job is lost, or job enjoyment or fulfillment can diminish. This happens. What can't happen is for managers to allow performance to drop below subpar levels as a result. When desire is lost and nothing makes a difference in that desire, it is time to take decisive action.

If the employee desires a transfer to some other job in the company, as a manager you might want to accommodate this request. However, accommodation should only be made if the past performance of the employee indicates a good track record. And the conditions of a transfer should include a period of time during which the employee gets his or her performance back on track. Under no circumstances should managers allow themselves to be held *at ransom* by the employee with poor performance as the leverage for transfer. If that is what the employee is doing, termination is the only alternative.

If performance and desire have dropped to a level at which the employee is clearly not a reliable asset to the organization or when the employee has consciously attempted to contaminate and disrupt other employees, a decision for termination must be made. In another organization, this employee may work out well. However, to keep a warm body around under these circumstances will damage management integrity and the performance culture of the organization.

Remember, when the situation gets to the point of termination, it is not the manager who is making the choice to terminate. The employee has *chosen* termination as a result of his or her behavior regarding performance. The *choices* that employees make create the *choices* that managers have. If the manager has been put in a corner with no way out as a result of the choices the employee makes, termination is the only alternative action. When it gets to this point, termination is in the best interests of all parties: the organization, the manager, other employees, and the terminated employee.

Leadership Action

When an outside problem exists or loss of interest in the job is apparent, the appropriate leadership action is again to *INQUIRE* into the source of difficulty, to *SUPPORT* by being as accommodating as possible under the circumstances, and to *ENFORCE* by ensuring that the required job performance standards be upheld or termination be required.

Performance Questions　　　　　　　**Leadership Action**

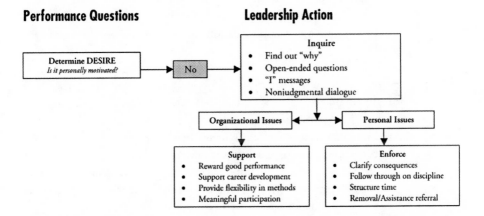

Here are some appropriate *INQUIRE, SUPPORT,* and *ENFORCE* actions when dealing with *personal issues…*

- When employees have the ability to perform at an acceptable standard yet do not put forth the effort necessary to perform with excellence:
    - ✓ Discuss and clarify the gap between the desired performance level and the present level.
    - ✓ Engage in open-ended questions to discover the reasons for the lack of effort.
    - ✓ Take a nonjudgmental stance in initially discussing the performance issues and reasons for the present state.
    - ✓ Use "I" messages to convey your feelings and understanding of the situation.
    - ✓ Get an understanding of the impact of the personal issue.
    - ✓ Offer accommodations in the short term to assist the employee in dealing with his or her issues (however, not at the expense of accepting poor performance).

✓ Direct employees to seek assistance via an employee assistance program when it is evident that their job might be in jeopardy due to their inability to handle a personal situation.

✓ Terminate those who no longer like their job or are bored to the extent that their performance is creating continued difficulties for the organization.

✓ Transfer those who seem unsuitable for their present job but have eligibility and suitability qualities for other jobs in the organization. The prerequisite is continued acceptable performance in the present job.

When personal issues become the cause of performance difficulties, the interventions are not usually enjoyable. However, the worse thing that can happen is for the manager to avoid an intervention. When employees, for whatever reason, fail to perform adequately, big problems can result and the negative impact on other employees can create difficulties that can be avoided with appropriate intervention in a timely manner. But remember, your intervention is a performance intervention...as a manager—not as a person who is trying to help employees "fix" their outside problems. That is a path you don't want to take. Stay with managing performance, your area of expertise.

CHAPTER 8

Initiative and Personal Responsibility

*"The more you get rid of your people's monkeys,
the more time you have for your people."*

—William Oncken, Jr.

Let's do a quick review. The first four questions and appropriate actions in the performance management process are the following:

- Are performance expectations clear?
  - Leadership Action: ESTABLISH
- Ability? Can the employee perform the task?
  - Leadership Action: TEACH

- Confidence? Does the employee have the confidence to perform on his or her own?
  - Leadership Action: ENCOURAGE
- Commitment? Are employees truly inspired to do their best? Do they participate in a meaningful way?
  - Leadership Action: INSPIRE
- Desire? Is the employee sufficiently committed and motivated to perform the task?
  - Leadership Action: INQUIRE ➔SUPPORT ➔ENFORCE

Once these questions have been dealt with and required leadership action has been taken where needed, the *desired state* in performance management has been reached. It is now time to ensure that employees have the initiative to take action.

- Determine Initiative (Does the employee have the responsibility to act or perform?)

The final stage in the process is ensuring that employees are not overly dependent on the manager but instead are in interdependent relationships—in which each employee becomes responsible for the initiative and results of his or her job duties.. This is achieved by ensuring that employees have the responsibility and initiative to perform their job and by applying effective delegation methods when people have learned their assignments.

Performance Questions   Leadership Action

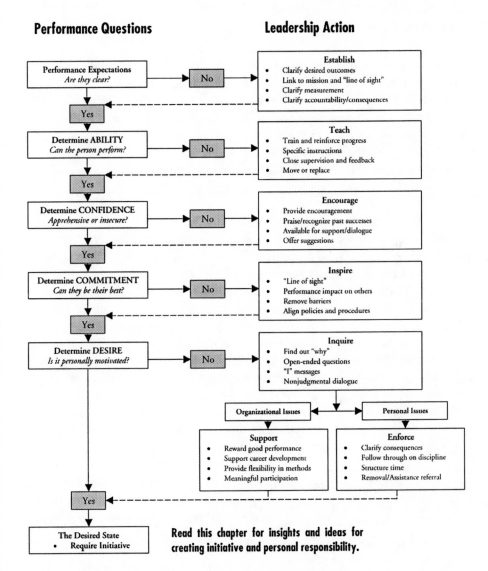

The Desired State
- Require Initiative

Read this chapter for insights and ideas for creating initiative and personal responsibility.

Managing Initiative

One of the best training courses we have ever attended occurred early on in our managerial life. The consequences of attending William Oncken, Jr's course on "Managing Management Time" were not only emotionally positive but radically changed our management approach. During the course of Mr. Oncken's seminar, we found ourselves wanting to share our own experiences. However, being averse to public humiliation and embarrassed by tearing up in front of peers, we resorted to laughter (albeit at myself) as we vicariously relived our managerial experiences through Bill's stories.

William Oncken, Jr., passed on in the late 1980s, but his legacy lives on with his seminars, delivered expertly by his son William Oncken, III, and his profound metaphor, "Who's Got the Monkey?" The late Mr. Oncken defined a monkey as the next step or action to be taken. In this parlance, whoever has the responsibility for performance at any time is the person who has the monkey.

Anyone who ever attended an Oncken seminar will never forget the managerial ineptitude in the following storyline: *"You are on your way to a meeting when approached by one of your employees. You are targeted with the line, 'Hey boss, we've got a problem.' As managers are programmed to be the ultimate problem solvers for their employees (after all what are bosses for?), you ask for an explanation. After receiving the brief overview, you realize that you don't have the time to deal with it at the moment. You cheerfully respond by saying, 'thanks for bringing that to my attention, I must get to my meeting and don't have time to give you an answer. I will get back to you.' You then go your way and the employee goes his or her way—the employee without the 'monkey' that arrived on his or her back and you with the 'monkey' you erroneously accepted with your response, 'I'll get back to you'!"*

Improper Initiative Transfer
This occurs when initiative for performance transfers from the party who should be taking it to a party who should *not* be taking it.

Along with Mr. Oncken, there have been many books, articles, and programs over the years dealing with creating responsibility and initiative. All take different approaches to arrive at the same conclusion: when initiative is transferred from one person to another in an organization and the person who takes initiative isn't the one who should be taking it, many harmful negative unintended consequences occur. Further, taking initiative away from people is nothing more than a rescue, with the consequences amounting to more harm than refusing to rescue.

The move from a work environment of dependency to one of personal responsibility is a necessity in today's competitive workplace. When managers are overwhelmed with answers employees need from them before work can proceed and when managers actually (consciously or unconsciously) hold up the work of employees, productive work and employee morale suffer. Moving to a performance environment where people are responsible for their own performance requires managers to become proficient at managing initiative, i.e., keeping the performance with the right person at all times.

Consequences of Misplaced Initiative

Managers take initiative away from their employees in many different ways. Some knowingly take initiative and then rationalize their action in the following way:

- "If you want it done right, do it yourself."
- "I've done it before, and I can do it better and faster."
- "I don't have enough time to let someone else work this out."
- "I don't want them to think I would have them do something I'm not willing to do."
- "My job is to save the day—if not, I wouldn't be the manager.

To be effective, managers must let go of these feelings. Let's put a stop to this nonsense right now. The first two rationalizations will continue to be a self-fulfilling prophecy for managers who continue to act on these notions. When employees don't have initiative, they will not learn to do things right, and they will not improve and get faster. Failure to grant performance initiative ensures the continuing cycle of robbing employees of their development and managers using up their time to do the work others could be doing. Regarding the third rationalization, if you don't have time to let others work things out, they will be forever dependent on you and you will lose time in the long run. The fourth rationalization is pure psychobabble, used when managers enjoy the gratification of doing what they are good at. Rarely have we ever seen this rationale applied to jobs in which the tasks are menial or routine or that managers dislike.

The last rationalization comes from the misplaced notion about the role of the manager. This rationalization is mainly egocentric, in that the manager enjoys the spotlight and the moniker of problem solver. These managers believe that saving the day is what earns them points in the organization and so it builds their own self-esteem. Well, *the Lone Ranger rides again!* The role of the manager is to develop talent so that *others* can save the day or even prevent the day from having to be saved at all. If the manager is the only one who can save the day and solve the problems,

> ### The Lone Ranger Rides Again!
>
> These are managers who mistakenly perceive their role as the responsible problem solver, the one who saves the day for all those who are helpless and denied the special talents of the manager. Egocentric and focused on himself or herself, the manager robs employees of opportunities to achieve, contribute, and maximize their talent and potential.

then the organization is being served poorly. Best to get the ego out of the way and allow others to learn the skills to solve problems and make decisions relevant to their jobs.

Additionally, some managers unknowingly take initiative away from others under the following notions:

- "It's a manager's job to be helpful."
- "It's a manager's job to be the problem solver."
- "It's a manager's job to be accessible."
- "It's the senior person's job to do better what he or she used to do"

Although well intended, these assumptions cause performance problems. Managers must reconsider these assumptions and understand how they really apply. Managers must be seen as helpful by employees. However, help cannot and must not be defined as doing for others what they can do for themselves. That is not help: it is welfare.

> *Employee Welfare Abuse*
>
> *Taking the performance initiative away from employees under the guise of being helpful, accessible, and solving problems.*

Managers must become adept at problem solving. However, regarding the work that others should be doing, problem solving takes the form of figuring out how to develop the talent within others so they can stand on their own two feet and solve their own performance problems.

Managers should be accessible to employees. However, access is not defined as performing functions and responsibilities that belong to employees. Access is being available to conduct the leadership actions in the Performance Advantage process and having the time to develop the talents of others. Becoming better at doing the work for which others are now responsible is not the pathway to managerial success. What got you the manager role is not what will allow you to win in that role. The transfer of talent from manager to employee is where the manager's talent and leverage manifests itself.

The consequences of wrongly placed initiative in an organization can be devastating. Doing the work for which others are responsible results in the following:

- Culture of employee dependency: dependent situations are not conducive to high performance or high self-esteem. When people can't stand on their own two feet and experience the fulfillment of self-achievement and contribution, they end up looking elsewhere for opportunities or just trade time for money; i.e., they quit and leave or quit and stay.

- Reduction of employee learning, development, and growth: when managers do the work that employees should be doing, no one develops or grows. The employees are cheated of the learning opportunities that lead to their development and growth. The managers, who already know how to do the job, gains nothing from the experience. No bench strength is created

- Elimination of employee creativity and innovation: managers will do the job or task the way they know how to, the way they do it best. Employees who aren't given the opportunity to develop their talents won't learn how to find better ways and won't even try, because their self-confidence will be usurped by managers who prefer to keep the initiative for themselves.

- Removal of employee responsibility: when managers do the work for others, the responsibility for the performance outcome lies with the managers, not with the employees!

- Destruction of employee performance accountability: when the manager does the work that employees should be doing, there is no one to hold accountable except the manager. The employee avoids any personal accountability because the manager takes the responsibility when he or she takes the initiative and does the work. This surely is not a desirable work culture.

- Renters of performance, not owners of performance: employees who have their initiative and responsibility taken away will not come to "own" the job. We are talking here about psychological ownership. We know that employees who feel they own their job significantly outperform those who feel they have no responsibility or accountability. Ownership, as well as effort, is transferred when managers take the initiative from employees.

- Limits personal productivity and excellence: without initiative and responsibility, employee performance will never reach its potential. The combined effects of dependency, lack of mastery, and misplaced accountability will erode the sense of achievement and contribution that employees must feel to motivate performance to its highest level.

> **Wrongly Placed Initiative**
> Results for employees
> - Creates dependency
> - Reduces learning, development, and growth
> - Eliminates creativity and innovation
> - Removes employee responsibility
> - Destroys performance accountability
> - Creates renters, not owners
> - Limits personal productivity and excellence
>
> *Other than that—not much harm done!*

These are consequences that will haunt managers and organizations for many years. To avoid these dilemmas, managers must become adept at resisting the temptation to lift initiative from the shoulders of employees and putting it on their own shoulders.

Keeping Initiative in the Proper Place

Resist the temptation to take the initiative from others. And it is a temptation. Let's go back and analyze the situation in the beginning of this chapter that Mr. Oncken uses to illustrate the transfer of initiative. There are five critical elements that all can influence a manager to take the poorly advised path, that is, taking the initiative for action away from the employee:

Here are some typical feelings the manager might experience in such situations:

- Stopped

  In the middle of something else, the manager has been brought to a halt with the attention-grabbing opener: *"We've got a problem."*

- Seduced

  The manager feels it is his or her job to be the problem solver and take personal responsibility for all problems within that area of activity because the employee often says, *"I know you know how to handle this."*

- Time trapped

  At the present moment, the manager does not have enough time to deal with the issue effectively or to make any decision and the employee even says, *"I know you are stuck for time."*

- Detail deficient

  In the present situation, the manager most likely doesn't possess sufficient information to make a decision or handle the issue effectively: *"I know you probably can't make a decision at the moment."*

- A pain reliever

  The manager does not like to see the pain and suffering of his or her employees and enjoys seeing the happiness and sense of relief in the employee as a result of taking the initiative: *"Thanks so much, boss; I knew you could help."*

The Result = *"I'll get back to you!"*

Now interestingly enough, that managerial response also creates *role reversal*. If the manager does not get back to the employee in a timely manner, the employee will most likely stop the manager or drop by the manager's office and offer the question, *"How's it coming?"* The employee is now checking up on and monitoring the performance of the manager regarding the quality of the manager's performance on the issue of *"I'll get back to you!"* If managers have several employees and they habitually take the initiative when employees could be taking it themselves, well, you can see the clamity

Craziness like this must be put to a stop. Whether it is unintentional or due to a misunderstanding of the role of manager, an overriding need for control, or a desire to be seen as helpful, managers must keep initiative in its proper place. Managers must end this cycle of dependency.

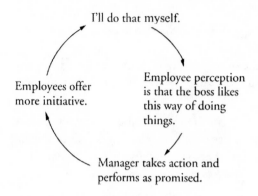

Initiative Transfer Trap

Taking the work that others should be doing, as a result of incorrect notions of the role of manager, the need for control, or the desire to be seen as helpful, creates a cycle of dependency on the manager.

Create a Cycle of Initiative

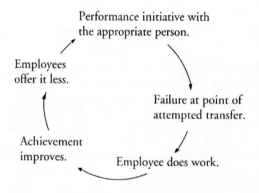

Cycle of Initiative

Not taking initiative from others, letting them do their own work, allows them to achieve more on their own, lessening their dependency on the manager, and to gain personal fulfillment from their own performance.

Using the process of the Performance Advantage Model, managers can take performance-based action with employees without taking away their initiative. When necessary, do the following:

ESTABLISH	• Provide clarity concerning goals, objectives, and areas of responsibility. Clean up any ambiguity, but make sure that the next performance step lies with the employee.
TEACH	• Provide structure and training when employees are in a learning curve. If show and tell is required, ensure that they are actively engaged in the demonstration and let them take over as soon as possible.

ENCOURAGE	• Provide encouragement when confidence is low but don't perform the work for the employee.
INSPIRE	• Remove obstacles that inhibit great performance, connect the dots so people can see the reason for their performance, and communicate the importance and relevance of tasks when commitment is low.
INQUIRE	• Ask questions to determine the cause of demotivation and lack of desire. Don't jump to conclusions regarding solutions or take action without determining valid causation.
SUPPORT	• Remove performance obstacles or alter policies and procedures where appropriate to allow employees to maximize performance—their performance!
ENFORCE	• Enforce appropriate rules and hold employees accountable for performance levels while ensuring that the initiative for performance remains with the employee.

As much as entirely possible, *never, never, never,* take initiative away from the employee. The ripple effect and the negative consequences to the organization are not worth the perceived short-term benefits. In conjunction with following the process of the Performance Advantage Model, put the following practices in place. Following these practices will ensure that a manager does not get trapped or seduced into taking the initiative in situations where responsibility for the performance initiative should not be changed.

Practices for keeping the initiative in the proper place:

(1) Ensure that employees bring performance difficulties or problems to you *before* you find out about them from another source.

(2) Have employees take the initiative to set up times to speak with you about problems or issues.

(3) Have employees collect all relevant information or data for any issue or problem being addressed.

(4) Make it a requirement that employees bring you all of the relevant data when conditions require you to make an on-the-spot decision that the employee is not authorized to make.

(5) Make it a requirement that employees do sufficient analysis and assessment of problems or issues; as a result, they bring you

• their best efforts in dealing with the problem or issue

• their best efforts at providing a recommended solution

(6) Require employees presenting a problem situation to identify the consequences to the business or organization resulting from the present way of doing things.

Keeping Initiative in Place

Direct employees to do the following:

✓ Come to you with performance difficulties or problems

✓ Take the initiative to set up discussions

✓ Collect relevant information and data

✓ Give best effort at analysis before coming to you

✓ Provide best effort recommendations

✓ Identify business consequences of present performance practices

Let them learn, develop, grow, and reach their full potential. Restore pride in the job and provide a sense of achievement and contribution to employees.

We recognize that there will be times when a decision is needed with little time to analyze information. In these situations, managers must reflect on whether the decision being brought to their attention is one that lies within their domain or one that could be made by the employee. Most often, we find that managers have created so much dependency that employees bring them the most mundane of decisions or don't even attempt to make decisions at the employee level. When managers hold themselves accountable to the managing initiative practices listed here, they find that—even when immediate managerial attention is required—employees provide relevant information and recommendations based on best effort analysis. It's only when employees are left off the hook, robbed of their responsibility, and stripped of initiative that managers are underprepared for *immediate* problem solving and performance management.

Initiative Where It Belongs

With initiative in the proper place, that is, belonging to the person whose job it is, a manager's overriding concern can be on results—the results that employees achieve through methods and performance practices which they develop themselves over time or by problem solving with their peers. When managers simply refuse to do the work of their employees, even at the risk of incurring short-run costs, employees are allowed to grow in terms of their ability and eventually are able to make most of the normal and routine decisions relevant to their jobs. When employee performance falls short of acceptable standards, managers can utilize the process in the Performance Advantage Model to uncover the cause and then take appropriate action without doing the job for employees.

Managers must refrain from taking performance initiative while maintaining a strong interest in the performance of others. The skill that managers bring to the table is the ability to ask the right questions, to be able to judge from the answers how employees think, and to teach employees the appropriate thought process so that they can solve issues and arrive at acceptable conclusions and recommendations on their own. Managers must not permit others to become dependent on them as the ultimate problem solvers. ever ready to prove their technical proficiency and perfectly willing to be Super Hero (see Lone Ranger) to subordinates in distress.

Super Hero

Managers who, misguided in their understanding of their role, feel compelled to demonstrate their personal technical superiority and expertise gained from past job experiences, doing better what they did before they were asked to develop the talents of others, thus denying others the opportunity to achieve equal success and self-confidence!

Managers must identify situations in which employees offer up their initiative for the taking as teaching opportunities. While being ultimately responsible for performance outcomes, managers must not take immediate responsibility for performance. The burden for performance and finding the solutions for improvement must lie with employees if talent is to flourish. Perhaps even more important, denying initiative to employees is to deny them the chance to develop their own problem-solving abilities and decision-making skills. The overarching benefit to the organization cannot be overlooked for the sake of pride over purpose regarding the role of the manager.

The Desired State: Require Initiative

When employees perform routinely at or above standard, managers should ensure that the performance initiative is with employees.

> **Require Initiative**
> * Never do what they should do
> * Provide questions, not answers
> * Require progress/learning reports
> * Hold accountable for initiative

Here are some appropriate *REQUIRE* actions for ensuring that performance initiative stays in the right place.

To keep initiative for performance with the employee and avoid taking their responsibilities:

* Never do the employees' work for them.
* Require best effort analysis or assessment when they bring situations to you for answers.
* Require best effort recommendations or possible solutions when they bring situations to you.
* Require an assessment of the consequences (positive and negative) of present performance conditions when discussing performance issues.
* Require reasoning that has been thought out thoroughly when employees *disagree* with your recommendations; don't settle for objections that are not based on facts.
* Require reasoning that has been thought out thoroughly when employees *agree* with you on ideas or recommendations; don't settle for agreement that is not based on facts or sufficient reason.
* When coaching performance, ask questions that require employees to think of alternatives and consequences; do not provide the answers.
* When coaching performance, teach your thought process; don't provide easy solutions that employees can mimic. *(Give them fish and they can eat*

today by relying on you; teach them how to fish and they can eat forever without dependence on you.)

- Require reports of no progress when discussing performance improvement efforts or performance status on projects or assignments.
- Be clear that help and assistance do not constitute doing another person's job.

Managing initiative is a critical step in the process of performance management. When initiative is misplaced, the negative effects for manager, employee, and organization are harmful and destructive. And proper initiative creates a platform for effective delegation—a practice of management that truly uncovers the talents of the manager and employee.

CHAPTER NINE

Delegation and Autonomy

"To the extent that leaders enable followers to develop their own initiative, they are creating something that can survive their own departure."

—John Gardner,
On Leadership

Delegation

When the desired performance stage has been reached with employees, the performance management situation calls for effective delegation. With understanding and mastery of the art of delegation, the success ratio of both managers and employees will go up. Both parties will experience less frustration with their jobs, and employee development and retention will be well served.

The benefits of effective delegation are well known and have been echoed in management books and journals for decades. Effective delegation allows managers to do the following:

- Achieve greater results with less personal and time involvement
- Achieve better cost effectiveness
- Provide job enrichment to employees
- Provide more opportunities for growth and learning to enhance employee career development
- Create a work environment reflective of personal responsibility and personal initiative
- Communicate trust
- Create higher morale in the workplace
- Improve time management
- Reduce the turnover of high performers
- Increase the productivity ratio per employee

Without effective delegation—that is, spending managerial time doing tasks that others could or should have been doing—the manager loses valuable time that could be spent on higher level responsibilities. The return on investment for learning effective delegation is worth the effort.

The prerequisite for effective delegation is to ensure that issues of the following are addressed and when needed, appropriate leadership action taken:

- Clarity around performance expectations
- Appropriate performance standards and measures
- Employee ability to perform the delegated tasks
- Employee confidence
- Employee commitment
- Employee motivation
- Employee initiative

We will address the topic of delegation slightly differently than most other authors. For many, delegation refers to additional tasks or projects outside the employee's normal job description that managers assign. We look at delegation as a specific managerial behavior in the performance management process. Thus, managers use delegation behavior for managing the performance of employee responsibilities within a job description as well as for the more traditional assignment of responsibilities and duties beyond the job description. In this context, we find most fitting Bob Nelson's definition in his remarkable little book, *Empowering Employees Through Delegation*.

"Delegation is defined as entrusting power and authority to a person acting as one's representative. During the process of delegating, employees are assigned tasks or responsibilities. They are given authority to complete the task, and they assume accountability for the completion."

Using this definition, we embrace delegation as transferring ownership of any job performance, responsibilities, and resultant consequences to the employee. For every element of job ownership that is established with the employee, the manager has time to take care developing the talent of other employees to bring them to the performance level at which delegation can be utilized. This is

Benefits of Effective Delegation

- Greater results with less involvement
- Better cost effectiveness
- Job enrichment for employees
- Opportunities for growth and learning
- Enhanced employee career development
- Personal responsibility initiative integrated into the work culture
- Trust communicated to employees
- Higher morale in the workplace
- Improved time management for managers
- Reduced turnover of high performers
- Increase the productivity ratio per employee

accomplished through the combined obligation of the manager and the employee: the manager has the responsibility to develop the potential of people in their job to perform at a level that does not demand constant management attention, and the employee has the responsibility to learn and perform his or her job at a level that does not require constant management attention. We believe that this mutual obligation should be communicated to all managers and employees at the moment of selection.

The Authority/Control Trap

When choosing to delegate, one of the biggest problems with ensuring reliable performance outcomes is the manager's failure to close what we call the "delegation triangle." To delegate effectively, the employee must not only have the responsibility to perform, but must also have the appropriate authority, combined with enough control over the process of the work to ensure the desired performance outcome. When one of the three is lacking, the performance outcome is at risk, through no fault of the employee.

We define authority as the degree of *influence* a person has over others when the performance of others is necessary to achieve desired results. We define control as the degree of decision making over *how* to perform a task or area of responsibility. When employees are responsible for meeting specific standards of performance and will be held personally accountable for their results, these two issues become of paramount importance. If these isssues are not addressed and then employees are held accountable, frustration, resentment, and eventually turnover or minimal work compliance are the results. Employees should not be held accountable for results that they had no authority to influence or for processes over which they had no control (when the existing process is a barrier).

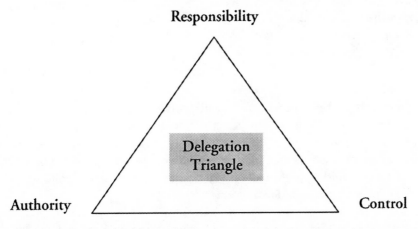

All three points of the triangle must be connected: the level of authority commensurate with the accountability for the specific area of responsibility and the amount of control necessary to achieve the desired or required performance results.

Chris Argyris, noted management scholar and routine contributor to the *Harvard Business Review*, gets right to the point…

> *"For companies to change, employees must take an active role not only in describing the faults of others but also in drawing out the truth about their own behavior and motivation. In my experience, moreover, employees dig deeper and harder into the truth when the task of scrutinizing the organization includes taking a good look at their own roles, responsibilities, and potential contributions to corrective action."*

When tasks are delegated to them, employees will most definitely scrutinize and come to understand the barriers to their success and potential contribution. When it becomes evident that they are responsible and accountable for results that they cannot achieve under the present circumstances (lack of authority or appropriate control), they see the manager and the organization as extraordinarily unfair.

Delegation Triangle

Assigning responsibility for a job, task, or project with the authority commensurate with the required performance accountability and the amount of control necessary to achieve the desired performance results.

Nothing is more unfair than holding people accountable for something they can't do. Yet, in their rush to extend personal responsibility and accountability in the organization, this is precisely what many managers have done and continue to do. We've asked workers, especially on the front line, to improve and to be accountable for their performance. In many cases, however, we've given them little control over the process (how they do their jobs), which is frequently the cause of most performance difficulties. In other words, the responsibility and accountability are present, but the individual employee's ability (affected by lack of authority and control) to meet them is absent. As a result, workers are often frustrated, customers are disgruntled, performance is not up to the desired level, and we rarely see the improvements we're looking for.

Thus, the first step in the process of effective delegation is to ensure that the authority and control issues are aligned with the responsibility given and accountability for performance results.

Reasons Managers Don't Delegate or Do So Poorly

There are numerous reasons managers refrain from using the management style of delegation with employees. Although many just don't know how to delegate effectively, for most, the reasons lie deeper in their assumptions about their role and the role of employees. Some of these reasons follow:

- Not wanting to give up control: The assumption is that managers have control and employees don't, combined with the mistaken notion that control is a finite commodity and that sharing control equals losing control.

- Seeing delegation as a loss of power: The belief that managerial power is vested solely within the managers themselves and not believing that empowering others increases power.

- The need to be in charge: An ego approach to the role of manager, which assumes that being in charge is the way to keep others in line (the Lone Ranger syndrome).

- Poor expectations of others: Having low expectations of the capabilities of employees; after all, if they were capable, they would be managers.

- The feeling of ultimate responsibility: Knowing that they have the overarching responsibility, managers do not want the performance of employees to be a factor in their own accountability.

- Enjoyment of doing what others should be doing: See the last chapter!

Although many of these reasons may seem legitimate, let's take a look at the truths hidden by these motives. First off, what control do managers really lose when they use a delegation leadership style with employees who have proven that they can perform at the desired standard? The only aspect of control that comes to mind (from years of practical management experience and from interviews with thousands of managers) is control over *how* the employee achieves the results. Why is that so important? There are many ways to achieve great results and talented people will find their special knack for getting superior results. Are questions of ethics and safety really an issue with good performers? If so, then the manager has a unique definition of what constitutes a good performer. Besides, legitimate rules and policies will keep people within the guidelines for ethical and safe behavior. What the manager gains is control over performance results because the good performers find ways to best utilize their talent and deliver results much better than they could by doing things exactly like their manager. People can't be better at being you than you can, but they can be better than you at being themselves. Go out on a limb; give the good ones a real chance to succeed.

The notion that "sharing power is equal to losing power" is an unfortunate one. Power is not a finite resource. Managers do not lose their power when their talented employees have the authority to act in behalf of the organization and the control to do the work in the best way they know how. However, many managers are "power mongers" who jealously hold onto every ounce of power for themselves as a precious commodity and retain all the authority to act. This behavior disenfranchises even the best employees and heads performance in a southerly direction. Effective managers know that the power given to good employees only enhances their power position in the organization. Nothing gives a manager more credibility and influence in an organization than having employees who, without intimidation or fear prompting them, turn out great results.

Power Mongers

Power mongers jealously hold onto every ounce of power for themselves and retain all the authority to act. This behavior disenfranchises even the best employees and heads performance in a southerly direction.

What does "being in charge" really mean? Shouldn't managers really dig down and attempt to understand what they are really in charge of? The notion that a manager is truly in charge of the behavior of others is naïve at best and most likely fool hearty. Although managers can control some aspects of wages and have control over recognition, rewards, and promotion opportunities, in the final analysis, employees are in charge of their own behavior. Effective managers understand that they are not in charge of people. They don't see employees as "my people." And most certainly, the employees don't run around telling everyone they "belong" to their managers. Both parties, managers and employees, are "charged" with achieving performance results. This can best be accomplished with talented employees who perform at or above standard and by managers who allow for some work autonomy, refrain from micromanaging what the employees do well, and provide them with a personal sense of achievement and contribution from their work efforts. Failure to delegate to good-performing employees results in managers being in charge of neither employees nor performance results.

We have known for years, from research and from real-life experiences, that the expectations a manager has in the potential of others manifests itself in the way that manager will treat people. And we also can predict with certainty that those expectations will turn into a self-fulfilling prophecy for the manager and the performance results that others

> *Self-Fulfilling Prophecy*
>
> *Management expectations of the potential and capability of others, turning into reality through the direct actions of the manager, as people are managed to the level of the expectations.*

achieve will be very close to what the manager expects. This phenomenon in organizational life cannot be overlooked. Managers can choose the expectations they have of the ability of others—high or low—and provide management action accordingly. The human capacity is served poorly by managers who carry low expectations about the potential and capability of others: they tend to never give anyone else the opportunity to excel.

Managers do have the ultimate responsibility for performance results. However, it is important for managers to distinguish between what delegation author Bob Nelson refers to as ultimate responsibility and immediate responsibility. This distinction is critical. While ultimate responsibility refers to the managerial accountability to see that all the assigned work is properly completed and that performance standards are met, the employee has the immediate responsibility for doing the work and completing it at the acceptable level. The employee who fails to perform adequately is responsible for that performance. The manager's responsibility refers to the management action taken in response to that failure and to the corrective action taken to get performance back up to standard. To fail to delegate using the doctrine of ultimate responsibility, managers would have to micromanage or do every performance responsibility under their purview; such a case is extremely unusual.

> **Reasons for Poor Delegation or Lack of Delegation**
>
> - Loss of control
> - Loss of power
> - Being in charge
> - Low expectations of others
> - Feeling ultimate responsibility
> - Enjoyment of doing what you do well

Many managers get to be managers by virtue of their superior performance at the very jobs they are now managing. Usually when people excel at things, they come to enjoy the things at which they excel. Not only that, the immediate feedback, gratification, and sense of accomplishment are what most people like to get from their work. The manager's dilemma is that he or she is now in the position of managing others doing the very work the manager is good at and enjoys. The manager does not get immediate feedback and gratification from the work of others: there is a time lag. The manager does not get the same sense of accomplishment reveling in the accomplishments of others as from doing the work personally. This leads to the temptation of "staying in the game" rather than coaching the game. To be effective, managers must understand that their role is to manage the performance of others and to take pride and gratification from the leveraging of their talents through the employees. This is truly what managers are paid to do. We believe that a short career in management awaits those who brag about still doing the work and not delegating effectively to others.

If Dogs Can Do It

At Morristown, New Jersey, lies a remarkable place: The Seeing Eye. Here they train dogs for sight-impaired handicapped people. The brilliant staff working with these amazing animals is something to behold. There are some interesting facets to the work done at this unique training facility. However, one stands out as worth addressing in this book.

The safety of the handicapped people is the paramount responsibility for these dogs. As such, it is imperative that they be trained to obey their masters. A disobedient seeing-eye dog would obviously be troublesome. So, what is the process? The dogs are all trained to *always* obey their masters—*unless they have a better idea!* That is, each dog is trained to

---

The Seeing Eye

This is a place where they train dogs to always obey their masters, unless the dogs have a better idea. The dog's paramount responsibility is to keep the master "in business." Crossing the street at the insistence of the master when a vehicle is entering the intersection is not in the best interests of the dog, the master, or the general public!

---

always obey unless the command will place its master in harm's way. In such cases, the dogs *must disobey*. This concept is so obvious that you wonder why it is not applied in organizations.

Imagine, if you will, the Seeing Eye applying normal employee training in their process. Consider the following:

> At the curb, the master, accompanied by the seeing-eye dog, is ready to cross. The master gives the command, *"Let's go"* to the dog. The dog looks and there is a truck coming towards the intersection. The dog mentions to the master that the decision to cross is not appropriate at this moment. The master, being the one in charge, says, *"I said, let's go."* The dog replies again that this order is not in the best interests of the master. The master, with more volume, asserts, *"Listen, I'm the boss here; now, let's go."* The dog, closing its eyes and gaining a vision of the future, thinks, *"Oh boy, what a bummer!"* Being polite, the dog offers an opportunity for the master to go first.

Of course, the dog must disobey: disobedience in this case keeps the master "in business." Why is it then that we ask employees to obey and follow the policies without thinking and to deviate under no conditions, even when confronted with situations in which following rigid and many times insane or stupid policies will drive customers away and be harmful to the business? After all, if dogs can be trained to use judgment in life-threatening situations, don't you think that people could be asked to do similar thinking when customer loyalty or coworker effectiveness or productivity issues are on the table?

> ### They Treat Us Like Dogs
> *Employees could be trained to obey and follow rules, unless the obedience and/or rules will result in harm for the organization, using their judgment in the process of performing their duties.*

We marvel at the tenacity of the dogs at the Seeing Eye. When confronted with a master who makes the mistake of giving a command that will be harmful, the dog will put tension on the leash, a sign that the command is unsafe. If the master persists, the dog will step in front of the master to impede progress. If this fails to do the trick, the dog will even get physical. There are hundreds of pounds of pressure in a German Shepherd's mouth, suggesting that the command which elicits a physical response from the dog is a very unwise rule!

With the art of delegation, we can capture the inspired and committed performance of most employees. The dignity, respect, and trust that come along with training and then allowing employees to use their judgment to work with excellence and simultaneously protect the financial, legal, or regulatory issues of the organization is worth its weight in gold. The return on the effort is employees who work with pride, self-motivation, and discretionary effort. If we don't learn to walk down this path more rapidly than we have in the past, well, if someone says, *"They treat us like dogs around here,"* we reply, *"You should be so lucky!"*

Closing the Loop

Many times the failure of delegation is the result of not closing the loop in the delegation process and thus creating anxiety and tension for the manager. For delegation to be successful, both the manager and the employee must get a sense of emotional security from the process. This doesn't happen when (1) the employee feels micromanaged in the process and (2) when the manager feels information deficient and out of control regarding the performance outcome.

Ironically, both of these emotions are created by failure to close the loop for those performance issues that receive a delegation approach. When managers feel out of the loop and out of control, when they don't possess current information regarding performance issues, when they are questioned from above, they expect the employee to fill the void. When this happens, the employee to who the task has been delegated may perceive that the manager lacks trust in his or her abilities and is really over managing the situation, not delegating. If the response to this situation by the employee is to withhold information or to withdraw, the manager's feelings and frustrations are only exacerbated.

Closing the loop will overcome these difficulties and help the manager achieve the desired results from his or her delegation efforts. The actions that managers can take to close the loop are the following:

- Support expectations: the level of support from the manager will provide what the employee needs to accomplish the desired results.
    - ✓ Give the employee the opportunity to decide what managerial support is needed.
        - Determine what situations call for managerial involvement.
        - If the "skids" need to be greased with other departments or senior people, agree on the manager's role.
        - If budget or funding issues are relevant, define the manager's role in the process.

- If barriers or obstacles must be removed or altered, what role does the manager play?

- Status reports and updates: the need for keeping the manager informed of performance status or progress.

  ✓ Determine how often the manager is to be informed of performance results or performance progress.

  ✓ Determine the timelines for required performance or progress updates.

  ✓ Require employee reporting of changes or problems as they occur; eliminate managerial surprises (learning about performance issues or problems from other sources).

  ✓ Require reports of no progress; on delegation of projects, ensure that, even when there is no progress, the manager is kept informed of the lack of progress and of the reasons for it (this ensures that questions won't go unanswered for too long).

- Define success

  ✓ Ensure that both parties, the manager and the employee, are mutually clear on the required performance outcomes, or results.

  ✓ Ensure that both parties re clear on the relevant timelines/deadlines that must be met.

Providing Autonomy

Use a delegative leadership style with those people who perform well. They have earned it. The most significant recognition a manager can give to a high performing employee is the autonomy and responsibility to stand on his or her own two feet. The communication of respect and trust that accompanies effective delegation builds pride, self-esteem, and inspired performance. Why would any manager who has an obligation to the success of any organization want anything less?

> ### Loose—Tight
> *Performance boundaries should be wide enough to allow the employee to handle all of the routine issues and predictable deviations that may come along while performing but, at the same time, narrow enough to protect the fiscal and liability responsibilities of the organization."*

For any task, assignment, or project, there are some critical steps for managers to follow when delegating work to employees and providing them with the autonomy to work on their own.

- Clearly communicate to employees what they are being asked to do and the standard of performance required (see Chapter 3).

- Describe the context and relevance of the work to be accomplished; it is important for employees to understand the importance of the work and how it connects to the overall success of the organization.

- Provide the authority necessary to influence others when their performance is necessary to achieve the required performance objective.

- Provide the necessary amount of control over the way things will be done to eliminate the possibility that the employee will prevented from accomplishing the goals due to procedures that are barriers.

- Close the loop by gaining clarity on the level of managerial support needed, gaining clarity on the types and frequency of status reports or updates necessary, and ensuring continued clarity about the required performance results and deadlines.

- Define the playing field: Let employees know the boundaries within which they must perform, the non-negotiable policies and work rules that must be followed. Real empowerment takes place within boundaries that allow for outstanding performance, not unstructured, ambiguous situations in which employees are left trying to figure out what is safe. The trick here is for the manager to define the playing field with boundaries that are *"wide enough to allow the employee to handle all of the routine issues and predictable deviations that may come along while performing but, at the same time, narrow enough to protect the fiscal and liability responsibilities of the organization."*

Remember, autonomy must be earned. However, once it is earned, failure to provide it creates a hindrance to superior performance and employee loyalty.

The Desired State: Delegate

When employees have earned, through their performance, trust and responsibility, the appropriate managerial action is to **DELEGATE.**

> ### Delegate
> - Delegate assignments and tasks
> - Provide authority and control
> - Empowerment and responsibility
> - Develop for future

Here are some appropriate *DELEGATE* actions when dealing with high performers.

- For ongoing tasks within an employee's job description:
    - Communicate specifically what you want accomplished.
    - Ensure understanding of outcome expectations.
    - Ensure clarity around the standard of acceptable performance.
    - Ensure understanding of how performance will be measured.
    - Communicate how often performance will be measured.
    - Agree on amount of autonomy and employee decision making.
    - Put the initiative on the employee for keeping the manager informed.
    - Hold employees accountable for results.
    - Use the Performance Advantage Model process to debrief any performance failures or difficulties.
- For projects or growth opportunities with tasks and assignments outside the employee's job description, use the actions just listed and include the following:
    - Communicate the importance and relevance of the assignment.
    - Provide appropriate authority to influence others when their performance is needed to accomplish the objective.
    - Provide the necessary control over the process (how the work is done) to ensure that there are no barriers to undermine the employee's efforts.
    - Decide on the amount of managerial support necessary.
    - Put the initiative on the employee for keeping the manager informed..
    - Ensure clarity concerning deadlines.

Effective delegation allows managers to leverage talent—their own and the talent of their employees. The process provided in this book is mostly common sense, peppered by years of practical managerial experience. Unfortunately, common sense is often *not* common practice. By applying the Performance Advantage Model as a process for performance management, managers give themselves and their organization a real performance advantage.

Author's Postscript

"Let us make clear one final prefatory point. We are not talking about mollycoddling. We are talking about tough-minded respect for the individual and the willingness to train him, to set reasonable and clear expectations for him, and to grant him practical autonomy to step out and contribute directly to his job."

—Tom Peters, *In Search of Excellence*

Diversity and Ethics

We recognize that many are working in multicultural workplaces. We deeply believe in the necessity for managers to learn the basic cultural characteristics that may disadvantage or hinder people in particular ethnic groups from succeeding at the level of their capability. Although we have not chosen to go into this issue in this book, the matter is still of significant importance.

It is an ethical responsibility for managers to understand when cultural issues are impeding performance and to provide help and assistance wherever and whenever necessary.

Making Performance Management Work for You

People's reactions to being introduced to a new game or activity bring about predictable responses. They first ask, "How do you play?" "How do you win?" "How do you score?" Whether it is bridge, soccer, softball, or Pictionary, the first thing that participants want to know is how to play the game and how to score. People demand to know how the success will be judged.

Once they understand the goals and the scoring, people quickly focus on the rules. What are the boundaries? What tactics are permitted and which are considered to be out of bounds? How do I play the game so I can score without being penalized? Before they can strategize, they need to know the limitations that restrict their actions.

The focus on goals, end lines, boundaries, rules, and limitations is a natural desire to understand the size and shape of the playing field to create predictability. If we were playing softball without clearly defined objectives and rules, the confusion would cause many to lose interest and quit. If the rules were so restrictive as not to allow some individual risk taking and sense of personal accomplishment, many would also lose interest and quit. In business, we won't stop playing—we are being paid. But that doesn't mean we won't lose interest and become bored. Without employee interest and commitment, performance excellence is impossible.

> ### The Game of Work
>
> • *How do I play the game?*
>
> • *What are the rules?*
>
> • *How do I succeed?*
>
> • *How will I be managed?*

As well as reacting to the performance management structure, people also want to know how they are going to be managed, to be coached. Much employee time and attention is given to trying to figure out the boss. As discussed, the way in which managers handle employee performance, combined with their expectations about the potential of others, has a tremendous influence on the type of performance employees give in response. The difference between compliance (performance that is at the minimal acceptable level) and commitment (performance that is the result of the discretionary efforts of employees) can most often be traced to the type of performance environment that the individual manager creates.

In other words, the primary role of leadership is to facilitate and inspire performance that produces organizational goals and objectives. The key to successful leadership is the application of a method to the performance management process. Like any other competency, a method allows for replication, reliability, critique, and continuous improvement. Without a method, leaders can't bring the discipline and rigor to leadership practices that result in more consistent, predictable, and successful outcomes. The Performance Advantage Method, a thoughtful decision-making process that can be incorporated into a leader's own personal style, provides a performance management system that is grounded in leadership and performance principles that correlate with high performance and employee retention and satisfaction.

The *Method* is founded on the following principles:

- Employee motivation: True motivation is a result of a work environment that allows for significant achievement, contribution, and meaningful participation.

- Performance expectations: A major cause of performance and motivation problems is unclear or misaligned expectations.

- Employee ability: If a person can perform to a standard if his or her life depended on it, then ability is present.

  ✓ Punishing or holding someone accountable for lack of ability is a poor leadership practice; for ability issues, teach and train.

- Employee commitment: If a person can perform to standard, then performance issues are the result of attitudinal issues: Sometimes confidence, sometimes desire or motivation.

> **Performance Advantage Underlying Principles**
>
> - Motivate: Provide opportunities for others to do good work
> - Clarify performance expectations
> - Teach to fulfill potential and capability
> - Earn employee commitment; don't settle for compliance
> - Create individual responsibility and initiative

  ✓ Confidence: Building confidence necessitates encouragement, support, recognition of success, and availability on the part of the leader.

  ✓ Desire/Motivation: If a person lacks desire or motivation to perform then the reason must be uncovered for positive resolution.

    - Organizational issues: When organizational issues such as restrictive policies, lack of recognition, lack of connection with mission, etc., are the issue, removal of these barriers is in order.

- Personal issues: When a dislike of the job, personal conflicts with others, lack of caring, etc. are the issue, consequence management is in order.

- Meaningful participation: When people demonstrate ability and a positive attitude, a collegial relationship with the leader that provides responsibility, learning, involvement, and empowerment increases performance and employee satisfaction and tenure.

- Leadership action: When the leader's action is aligned with the follower's performance results and attitude (and not on the leader's comfort zone), performance, retention, and relationships improve.

What will your performance culture be? What stories will people in your organization tell about how they are managed and led? What stories will people tell about poor performers? What stories will people tell about excellence and whether or not the effort is worthwhile? The culture is in stories, not the manuals and not on the posters!

> *"Procedure manuals might have rules, but stories have morals. The latter tend to influence thinking and action more than the former."*

> —Bob Waterman
> *The Renewal Factor*

Next Steps

Today, organizations are being challenged by two intersecting forces: each organization's search for value and each individual's search for identity. In this equation, the manager is the catalyst. Its true, the manager does in fact define and pervade the employee's work life. The manager is the critical player in building a high performance workplace.

Effective managers know their role, to unleash the human spirit by developing the unique talents of each employee. This role is best played one on one, manager with employee, listening, dialoging, coaching, and respecting.

Consider then the following: when asked, most managers in organizations state that the ***most important*** and influential aspect of their performance management process is the face-to-face performance discussions between employees and managers. When asked, "What is the weakest part of your performance process?" managers answered, "the face-to-face performance discussions!" Organizations have a critical need when a *most needed* skill is also the *weakest skill.*

To be effective in the process of performance management, managers must develop effective performance coaching and communication skills. However, managers must begin to admit a skill deficit. When asked, most managers will reply that their communication skills are *well above average*; 80% of managers rate themselves in the top 10% regarding effective performance communication with employees! Not only does the math not compute, but when observed, the communication skills of most managers are not developed to the extent necessary to manage the performance of others effectively.

To go further with the Performance Advantage Model, we offer our new book coming in the early spring, *Face to Face: The Coaching Advantage.* This performance coaching process will provide managers with the insights and skills to get all of the pertinent and relevant information when asking the performance questions contained in the Performance Advantage Model. With understanding and practice, managers can gain the coaching and communication competencies that are an integral part of their managerial role and that build performance management expertise.

We certainly hope you enjoyed reading our book. After years of managing people, dealing with the successes and difficulties that come with management responsibilities, and the experiences we have had with so many organizations that daily face the challenge of gaining a performance advantage in the marketplace, we wanted to present the lessons we have learned. We believe much to be common sense. We hope those who have taken the time to read this book will also take the time to put common sense into common practice.

There is untapped potential in the workplace. And you, the manager, are the catalyst!

Thank You, **Rick Tate & Julie White**

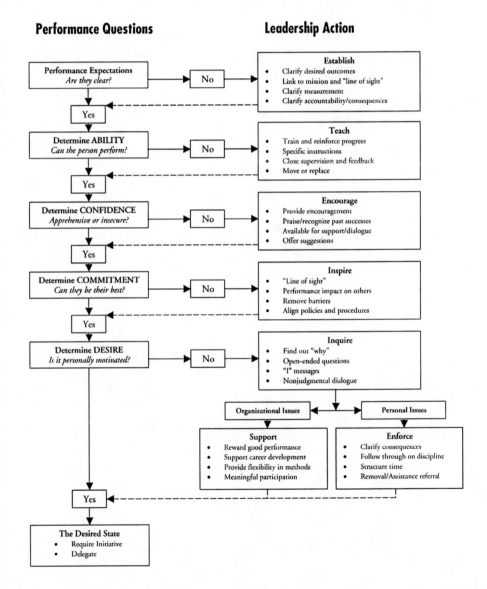

Performance Questions

Performance Expectations
Are they clear? → No

Yes ↓

Determine ABILITY
Can the person perform? → No

Yes ↓

Determine CONFIDENCE
Apprehensive or insecure? → No

Yes ↓

Determine COMMITMENT
Can they be their best? → No

Yes ↓

Determine DESIRE
Is it personally motivated? → No

Yes ↓

The Desired State
- Require Initiative
- Delegate

Leadership Action

Establish
- Clarify desired outcomes
- Link to mission and "line of sight"
- Clarify measurement
- Clarify accountability/consequences

Teach
- Train and reinforce progress
- Specific instructions
- Close supervision and feedback
- Move or replace

Encourage
- Provide encouragement
- Praise/recognize past successes
- Available for support/dialogue
- Offer suggestions

Inspire
- "Line of sight"
- Performance impact on others
- Remove barriers
- Align policies and procedures

Inquire
- Find out "why"
- Open-ended questions
- "I" messages
- Nonjudgmental dialogue

Organizational Issues ← → Personal Issues

Support
- Reward good performance
- Support career development
- Provide flexibility in methods
- Meaningful participation

Enforce
- Clarify consequences
- Follow through on discipline
- Structure time
- Removal/Assistance referral

"Hooks"

To connect important ideas and concepts for your immediate recall.

People leave managers…not organizations
- The relationship between the manager and the direct report is the significant variable that affects employee productivity and retention. The use of sound leadership and management principles has a profound impact on the organization.

Lone Ranger Leadership
- Individualistic, authoritarian, has all the answers. creating dependency in the followers.

Pink Pills
- The manager's comfort zone when managing and leading people. What feels comfortable and successful to the manager is what is normally applied to employees regardless of the different performance needs of each employee.

Beer Bust and Softball
- The knee-jerk reaction to motivating people through a bribe. It rejects the notion that there is most likely something in the work environment itself that restricts and inhibits people's talents and efforts.

I Mean You No Harm
- A prerequisite condition in the workplace necessary to influencing high performance. Managers must make an obligation to ensure that trust, respect, dignity, fairness, equity, and sincerity are present in workplace.

The Law of the Hog

- Predictable employee behavior as a result of mistreatment and nonparticipation.

Whale of the Month

- Recognition programs that create cynicism, destructive competition, and are not focused on performance.

Five on Five

- The process of manager-employee performance expectation alignment.

65 mph Speed Limit

- Accountability creates consistent clarity for performance expectations and is an important element of a motivating work environment.

Line of Sight

- Connecting what each individual employee does to its ultimate impact on other human beings.

Cause Worthy of Commitment

- Performance expectations connected to a purpose beyond financial success and performance appraisal.

I Don't Know. I Just Work Here.

- Employees who don't know why things are done they way they are, leaving others frustrated and dissatisfied with their performance.

One Size Fits One

- Acknowledgment of the individual personalities and talents of employees and providing them with the opportunity to maximize their individual potential. Focusing on the outcomes, not the means, promotes personal talent.

Define the Playing Field

- Create behavioral values that dictate *how* employees perform their duties.

Suitability

- Behavioral preferences and willingness to "play well with others" and perform job tasks well that makes an employee a fit for the job and the organization.

The First Date
- What you get during the first thirty days regarding attitude is normally the best you will see. Wishing and hoping for future improvement rarely pays off.

Managerial Malpractice
- In medicine, it is malpractice to prescribe and *take* action without accurate diagnosis of cause. In managing the performance of people, sadly enough, failure to identify cause accurately is merely commonplace.

Bowling with No Pins
- This is the effect of a lack of connection between work efforts and contribution to the goals and objectives of the organization. The result is the employee activity of "trading time for money!"

Touch the Stove
- Managers need to experience the consequences of their actions and decisions that affect how employees perform to gain an understanding of what things support performance and what things don't!

Deflators
- Managerial pronouncements that lack explanation and relevant facts; they disenfranchise the mind and kill the human spirit.

Freeway Noise
- Management noise that ultimately contains no consequence, positive or negative, and gets tuned out due to the continual, mind-numbing reoccurrence combined with lack of follow through!

Transfer the Problem
- Management tactic of avoiding confronting performance problems by transferring or promoting the poor performer. This sends the message, "Screw up and get what you want!"

Can't Afford to Lose You
- Management tactic of refusing to promote or transfer their best people, thus sending the message that superior performance and extra effort will get you nowhere.

Employee Welfare Abuse
- Taking the performance initiative away from employees under the guise of being helpful, accessible, and a problem solver.

Initiative Transfer Trap
- Taking the work that others should be doing as a result of incorrect notions of the role of manager, the need for control, and the desire to be seen as helpful, creating a cycle of dependency on the manager.

Cycle of Initiative
- Not taking initiative from others, letting them do their own work, allowing them to achieve, lessening their dependency on the manager, gaining personal fulfillment from their own performance.

Super Hero
- Managers who, misguided in their understanding of the role of manager, feel compelled to demonstrate their personal technical superiority and expertise gained from past job experiences, doing better what they did before they were asked to develop the talents of others, denying others the opportunity to achieve equal success and self confidence!

Delegation Triangle
- Assigning responsibility for a job, task, or project with the authority commensurate with the required performance accountability and the amount of control necessary to achieve the desired performance results.

Power Mongers
- Managers who jealously hold onto every ounce of power for themselves as a precious commodity and retain all the authority to act. This behavior disenfranchises even the best employees and heads performance in a southerly direction.

Self-Fulfilling Prophecy
- Management expectations of the potential and capability of others, turning into reality through the direct actions of the manager, as people are managed to the level of the expectations.

They Treat Us Like Dogs
- Employees who are trained to obey and follow rules unless the obedience and rules will result in harm for the organization. using their judgment in the process of performing their duties.

Loose—Tight
- Performance boundaries wide enough to allow the employee to handle all the routine issues and predictable deviations that may come along while performing but at the same time narrow enough to protect the fiscal and liability responsibilities of the organization.

The Game of Work
- Questions employees want answered:
  - How do I play the game?
  - What are the rules?
  - How do I succeed?
  - How will I be managed?

Classic References for Effective Performance Management

To learn more about leadership and management skills, we recommend the following:

Blanchard, Kenneth, and Spencer Johnson. *The One Minute Manager.* New York, NY: Morrow, 1982.

Buckingham, Marcus, and Curt Coffman. *First, Break All the Rules.* New York, NY: Simon and Schuster, 1999.

Fournies, Ferdinand R. *Coaching for Improved Work Performance.* New York, NY: McGraw-Hill, 2000.

Heil, Gary, Rick Tate, and Tom Parker. *Leadership and the Customer Revolution.* New York, NY: Van Norstrand Reinhold, 1995.

Hersey, Paul and Kenneth H. Blanchard. *Management of Organizational Behavior*, 8th ed. Englewood Cliffs, NJ: Prentice Hall, 2001.

Kouzes, James M., and Barry Z. Posner. *The Leadership Challenge*, 3rd ed. San Francisco, CA: Jossey-Bass, 2002.

Linden, Russ. *Working Across Boundaries.* San Francisco, CA: Jossey Bass, 2002

Mager, Robert F., and Peter Pipe. *Analyzing Performance Problems.* 2nd ed. Belmont, CA: Lake Publishing, 1984.

Massey, Morris. *The People Puzzle.* Reston, VA: Reston Publishing, 1979.

McGregor, Douglas. *Leadership and Motivation.* Cambridge, MA: The M.I.T. Press, 1966.

Miller, Lawrence M. *American Spirit: Visions of a New Corporate Culture.* New York, NY: Morrow, 1984.

Nelson, Robert B. *Empowering Employees through Delegation.* New York, NY: Irwin, 1994.

Nelson, Robert B. *1001 Ways to Reward Employees.* New York, NY: Workman, 1994.

Oncken, William, Jr., *Managing Management Time.* New York, NY: Prentice Hall, 1984.

Shriver, Sam. *From Coach to Coach.* Escondido, CA: Fulcourt Press, 1989.

Taylor, Harold L. *Delegate: The Key to Successful Management.* Toronto, Canada: Stoddart Publishing, 1989.

Tichy, Noel M. *The Cycle of Leadership.* New York, New York: Harper Business, 2002.

Rick Tate & Julie White Ph.D. are Managing Partners of Impact Achievement Group, Inc.

For Information regarding how you and your organization can benefit from breakthrough methods, activities, and materials on:

- Leadership
- Customer Loyalty
- Performance Management
- Workshops
- Keynotes
- Consulting
- Simulations & eLearning

Contact:
Impact Achievement Group, Inc.
info@impactachievement.com
Toll Free: 888-248-5553
Phone: 425-885-5940
Fax: 425-558-1141

0-595-33168-8